T0191432

*Secrets to Moving Forward after a
Marriage That Defined You*

the

high school

sweetheart's

survival guide to

uncoupling

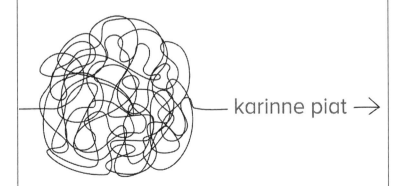

karinne piat $\rightarrow$

The High School Sweetheart's Survival Guide to Uncoupling
Secrets to Moving Forward after a Marriage That Defined You

Difference Press, Washington, D.C., USA
Copyright © Karinne Piat, 2019

All rights reserved. No part of this book may be reproduced in any form without permission in writing from the author. Reviewers may quote brief passages in reviews.

ISBN: 978-1-68309-240-7

No part of this publication may be reproduced or transmitted in any form or by any means, mechanical or electronic, including photo-copying or recording, or by any information storage and retrieval system, or transmitted by email without permission in writing from the author. Neither the author nor the publisher assumes any responsibility for errors, omissions, or contrary interpretations of the subject matter herein. Any perceived slight of any individual or organization is purely unintentional. Brand and product names are trademarks or registered trademarks of their respective owners. The information, ideas, and recommendations contained in this book are not intended as a substitute for medical advice or treatment.

Cover Design: Jennifer Stimson
Editing: Moriah Howell
Author's photo courtesy of: Ben Geier

DP
DIFFERENCE
PRESS

To Ben. It is with honor and gratitude to you that I write this book. I am blessed to have shared a life with you, and to have uncoupled with grace, kindness and authenticity. May it be payed forward in service to those of us struggling to do the same.

TABLE OF CONTENTS

FOREWORD

Dear reader,

If you've found your way to these pages, you've likely recently separated or divorced from your spouse and high school sweetheart. Let me first reassure that you will find solace in this work. You may be heartbroken and confused. Your heart may be aching and your mind spinning. Your heart-mind connection may be totally out of sync or incoherent. But do not despair because you had enough faith, hope, and courage for a better tomorrow to pick up this book, The High School Sweetheart's Survival Guide to Uncoupling. Perhaps providence played a role in directing you to this space or a kindhearted friend or a loved one purchased this guide for you. Whatever your path, here you are; you stand at the crossroads of the life-song full of blessing and fulfillment you planned from birth and an alternative path that seems to fall woefully short of your dreams and aspirations.

Today you can hardly imagine a life with no more sorrow, tears, or pain from the splintered relationship and/or broken promises. Yet here you are looking to transform your life into one of authentic power where heart, mind, and soul are in alignment; you are ready to live in harmony, cooperation, love, and reverence. What I'm describing may sound like "heaven on earth," but let me assure you that this blissful existence is within your grasp. With the purchase of this book comes the blessing of choosing Karinne as your spiritual guide and coach on this new voyage of discovery as you traverse this stormy yet passable sea.

I've known Karinne for over seven years at this writing. I sought healing in a massage with Karinne after I completed a marathon in April, 2012. My muscular structure was as tight as a drum after that marathon. With hindsight, I know now that my spirit and psyche were equally inflexible and defensive at that time. Let me try to describe that first healing encounter to the best of my ability. It is my hope that relaying some of my experiences will give you insight into Karinne's essence, divine gifts, and calling. Perhaps it may help establish her qualifications as a healing authority worthy to be your restorative guide and coach.

I arrived at the appointed time to Fox River Pilates and was met by a beautiful, petite, and vivacious (full of life, spirit) young woman. She escorted me to her sacred healing room along the river and had me lay comfortably on my back on the massage table. She turned on some soothing music and told me to relax and be present by emptying myself completely, particularly my mind and heart, through focused breathing. I closed my eyes, focused on the rhythm of my breath as best I could and waited as she slowly circumnavigated the table with both hands outstretched 6 to 12 inches from my body. I had never received a massage before, so I began to be a little apprehensive and silently and impatiently thought, "If this is a massage, then I want my money back!" Soon after Karinne said, "You have wonderful energy and spirit. Would you like to try Craniosacral Therapy (CST) instead of a traditional massage?" She explained CST to me. I didn't get it, but nonetheless let go and trusted Karinne's judgment. A long-term pattern of letting go and trusting Karinne's intuition and guidance quickly developed hereafter.

Please let me quickly digress at this point to explain CST a little further as I think it is particularly important in understanding Karinne's gifts. According to the Upledger Institute International website, CST was pioneered and developed by osteopathic physician John E. Upledger at Michigan State University, where he served as a clinical researcher and Professor of Biomechanics. CST is a gentle, hands-on method of evaluating and enhancing the functioning of a physiological body system called the craniosacral system - comprised of the membranes and cerebrospinal fluid that surround and protect the brain and spinal cord. Using a soft touch generally no greater than 5 grams, about the weight of a nickel, practitioners release restrictions in the craniosacral system to improve the functioning of the central nervous system. For more information on

CST, please also see *The Heart of Listening, A Visionary Approach to Caniosacral Work* by Hugh Milne. Karinne studied and trained at the Upledger Institute for certifications in CST as well as SomatoEmotional Release (SER) thus stepping into her inter-dimensional adept healing gifts as she retrieved, released and transformed buried energetic trauma within the body's tissues. She also attended the trainings of Janet Oliver, studying fundamental reflex integration and neuroplasticity and applied methods to rewire and fix dysfunctional mind-body patterns using the HANDLE approach. But perhaps the most influential training she received occurred at age 10 from her grand-mother Cynthia Ploski, a spiritual artist and author of *We, The Arcturians: A True Experience, Conversations with My Healers: My Journey to Wellness from Breast Cancer, and Chasing the Magdalene*. Karinne recalled with a gentle smile the day her grandmother opened her eyes to see the glowing auras around her hand and showed her how to feel and move energy through her hands to heal others. She noted that this was the day she felt the calling to be a healer. This beginning of cultivating vision, healing, intuition and her profound love for mankind has shaped her life from an early age. This is quite obvious in the uniqueness of her presence, her observations and within the stories of life she shares.

Let's return now to that first CST session. Karinne moved to the end of the table and delicately and skillfully cradled my head to perform CST. What soon followed was an auspicious and ineffable mystical experience. I recall discussing her gentle yet powerful healing hands after the session and associating the sensory experience to biblical laying on of hands. I journaled about a subsequent CST session as follows: "I had this incredible feeling like breathing for the first time, totally awake and alive yet relaxed, and a deep feeling of peace/bliss (full of grace)." Maybe now you can begin to understand from whence my earlier references to "heaven on earth" were derived.

After these and other similar uplifting experiences over the past several years, I've come to fully recognize Karinne's deep compassion, motherly tenderness, courage, loyalty, empathy, loving kindness, and concern for others. I think the one word that perhaps best describes Karinne's unique essence is valkyrie. The term valkyrie ("choosers and helpers of the fallen") comes from Norse mythology. These female angels or spirits escorted the worthiest of the fallen Norse warriors to Valhalla, or heaven, where these gladiators enjoy divine life with the gods. I think a listen to Richard Wagner's triumphant "Ride of the Valkyries" composed in 1870 may give you an "audio-biography" of Karinne to ponder. This operatic prop may be useful in making Karinne spiritually present with you in lieu of physical presence as you do the important work of instilling Karinne's words of wisdom and encouragement, stories of her successful epic voyage through troubled waters, and soothing invocations imparted within this book.

I have one last story that wonderfully encapsulates Karinne. I need to shroud some important facts in mystery since Karinne will give her account later in this guidebook. Let's just say that the episode involves an irresponsible and violent affront to her family's home and well-being by a troubled stranger. Rather than responding with anger and vengeance to this interloper, Karinne extended love and compassion and comforted the intruder until the authorities arrived. I believe that this remarkable act of mercy has been praised in Valhalla and on earth.

I'd like to close this forward by offering a blessing for you to recite. It is a healing prayer from Catholic.org that I often say at Adoration and other sacred places.

Lord, look upon me with eyes of mercy, may your healing hand rest upon me, may your lifegiving powers flow into every cell of my body and into the depths of my soul, cleansing, purifying, restoring me to wholeness and strength for service in your Kingdom.

May God be with you,

John S. Heneghan Servant Financial, Ltd., an investment advisory firm in Aurora, IL Oblate of Marmion

Abbey Extraordinary Minister and Adorer of the Eucharist, Holy Angels Parish

CHAPTER 1

Facing Divorce

Young love. I am of the belief that young love is of the purest and most profound. Did you get any validation for your love when you were young? I didn't. In fact, I hid it. I knew it wasn't accepted. I was told I didn't know what love was. What a bizarre, culturally acceptable statement, and how utterly untrue. To find your future spouse in childhood has unique advantages and disadvantages. I thought it best to write an uncoupling book speaking directly to those who experienced this, and who, in my opinion, are quite misunderstood in the beginning of their relationships. This is followed by having marriages that are at times overly-romanticized and idealized, often crediting unusual good luck to your happy union. And, in the moment where all becomes public that you are facing divorce, the trust and belief in the meaning behind your togetherness, once a stone sculpture divinely crafted, crumbles. The tumbling rocky chunks land in a sort of rubble that resembles the original broadly culturally acceptable misunderstandings that once again invalidate your love. "You got married too young," they say. "You just grew apart," as if implying that it was eventual should you develop any interests along the way. And my personally least favorite statistic meant to shed some sort of light on your situation, "Well, over fifty percent of marriages end in divorce," in my mind, code for "half of marriages are failures."

It is in the face of divorce that I would like to provide a voice that understands what others will not. One that can guide you in how to handle this very awkward time after you separate, the devastation of losing family and friends instantaneously when you've known them forever, and, even worse, the thoughts of what critical views and judgments of you they may have. You may be worried about all the things you have to let go of, which may include your home, the school your children attend, pets, and time with your children, not to mention the very uncertain idea that divorce is, in fact, the way you should move forward. It's difficult not to have the support of a voice that knows. There are a lot of people who love you, but who can really hold space for what you are going through? Let us always open up to the people who love us, our dearest friend or our mother,

2

and allow them to reach their limits of personal experiences in their consoling of us, accepting the warmth of their intentions.

The monster under your bed is the feeling of losing your family along with your husband, the man with whom you've spent nearly your entire life. Let's not pretend that you can't feel the silver lining in this, because there were aspects of your marriage that were infinitely difficult, but the idea of divorce is terribly unsettling. In the back of your mind, it's hard to reconcile the amount of effort it will take to complete this total separation. Your future, once vivid, incrementally has been bleaching out the last few years, and here you are, in the whiteness, crying out because it's all too sad and all too scary. It's a very multifaceted situation, and your dearest friend or your mother, who is at the other end of the line, as much as she tries to comfort you, can only come from her own perspective – and her words don't always provide the comfort you would so love to have. You get off the phone. The drive home would be quiet if not for your sobbing.

Where do you go from here?

Home. You go home because that's what's next. You live day to day, moment to moment. Everything is totally the same and yet completely different. In the days after your relationship ended, everything has changed. Your family, which included all of your husband's side, whose numbers may have far outnumbered your own, are now no longer your family like they were. Even worse is that you worry they blame you. "I hope she comes to her senses," you hear through the grapevine. And with that, a solid pang to the stomach.

As you make hushed phone calls to your parents, siblings, and friends to let them know that your relationship ended, they make their various assumptions. Your relationship that once felt private and personal can be put through a phone line and dissected to the satisfaction of others' need to answer why. The why is a deeply personal subject. There are a few people you will even consider going into to the real details with. It often seems the better choice to give them a vague reply and let them come up with their own false reasons. None of this static noise of misunderstanding is really at the heart of your pain, though. It's the ending of your life you most caringly put together. It's the family you started ... this family life was central to your life's plan. It expresses who you are at the core. It served as the foundation for all things to come. There is so much at stake that it's difficult to know what to do. How do you know that divorce will be the best solution? Even if you were the one who was forced to throw in the towel, how often are there moments that call your words back to question? Given the complexity, if you try to answer, then you're in for a spinny ride. Things easily get very confusing. As you stand here on the threshold of divorce with your childhood sweetheart, there are a lot of important questions you will be asking yourself and your spouse. Questions that you must find the truth to. You must find your way because it means everything. When you made your vow, you meant it, every word, for life. So, for something to come up that challenges that, it must be pretty goddamned important.

So, we stand squarely in this most pivotal moment, a position that requires so much care and tenderness, keen senses and intuition, and coming from a place of heart – not insecurity. It is easy to be enveloped in anger, defend yourself in every conversation, or lie in a bed of self-pity, covers up over your head, wet tear-filled ears. I have endless compassion for these miserable moments of despair. Yet, it is out of love that I remind you that we cannot allow ourselves to act from a powerless state, especially not now. Your future depends on it. You know well the consequences should you never take hold of this sword of strength. You probably know it from your very own upbringing. What story do your parents have? How did you feel about it and what had you decided for your own family? We also hear our family members, friends, and acquaintances' maundering on unhappy relationships and fuming about self-interested ex-partners in their lengthy painful divorces. Do you know someone going through an upsetting divorce now? Have you sensed how their children suffer? You'd have to sense it, because children don't wear their hurts on the outside.

5

They keep their pain deep, deep down in the speechless core of their being. It finds its way through cracks and crevices, every once in a while erupting when the surface situation merits a nice upheaval, and then the molten emotion can spill forth and release such inner tension. Parents handling the difficulties of divorce will with certainty at one time or another miss their children's gulping of such distress. However, if you can hold space for a peaceful and, dare I say, loving uncoupling, you can catch a few heaping mouthfuls before they're swallowed down. The loving attitude of the attuned parent lessens the exterior tension and stress of the uncoupling process for everyone, and so greatly softens the child's experience, creating space to more easily digest their emotions. After all, in choosing a loving divorce, you have the mental wherewithal to often check in with children and pick up on their well-being.

What is most important (and has always been most important) is the emotional wellness of everyone in your pod. You search for every possible solution to make room for what each person needs, and, most recently, you are willing to demand with fervor what it is that you need too. This could be a rather new voice you've recently found. Ignore your own needs long enough and your heart will scream in such a pitch that it blocks your ability to hear much else – and, finally, you must pay attention. It seems like your life depends on it.

It does.

Tell me you have reached a moment like this in your life, when all the power in your brain and body could no longer hold you back from using your voice to say what you need. The levee was no longer able to withstand the pressure of the heart's emotional waves, and the strength of this underlying current crashed through the barriers the day the real you set out to reclaim itself. Speaking out for your own needs has powerful implications, as does the deluge busting through the levee and cascading wildly forward, rushing over manmade structures and arriving in new plains. It sends a ripple through your life, touching everything and everyone, changing you forever. There's no apologizing here. The cyclical floods bring fertile soil, and should a relationship embrace this pathbreaking potential, one could stay pointed firmly in the direction of the stars. This new expansion of self brings the promise of fullness and pleasure yet to be experienced. Once you feel the possibilities and potential, you can never shrink your spirit back to fit the old size and shape. In the moments that you found yourself in new ways you love, know that this vibrance is yours to keep forever. There may be times when the situation doesn't seem to allow you to dance as freely as you had, and if the days stretch into years, you may forget it all together. Despite what you think, the joy has not been lost in the storm that surrounds you. Rather, it resides safely within you.

Beneath the whipping winds of sadness and bewilderment is the knowledge that your future does exist. There is more personal expansion waiting for you on the other side that pulls you energetically forward. While you ask yourself where you go from here, pulling up into the driveway of your tempestuous house once again, you know that one day you will be in the driveway of a new home, that one day you will arrive in your new life, and that the whiteness that is your future, will fill in. While acknowledging the many fears that invade this thought, I approach the future with a healthy amount of fascination. Where you will go from here is so very much determined by your own unique magnetism, forces that animate you and connect you. You may be aware of these energies generated within or look to influence them, but inevitably your future will meet you at every moment, starting with exactly where you are now. What do you want in your life? What do you want it to feel like? How curious is it to look into the white and know that your future will come forward to meet you right where you stand! How do you move forward from here, keeping the things you love and giving you more of what you need? This is something I'd like to focus on and explore with you in this book.

You have a decision to make. This decision is much more far-reaching than you might have considered. Obviously, you have a hand in how difficult the immediate road ahead of you will be. How you play into the drama and how you respond to your partner through this process will place your comfort on a scale anywhere from meaningful and heartfelt to excruciating and agonizing. What you may not realize is that how you uncouple lays the foundation for so many years after the divorce is over and final. Unknowingly, you are deciding how to set the stage for your next life to play out, with your children, for yourself and for your relationship with your future ex-spouse. If you continue to think short-term and miss what lies beyond the tip of your nose, you waste the very preciousness of your children's growing years that passes all in an instant. The stress of your divorce can easily cause your children to act out and tantrum, their grades to drop, their friendships to suffer and they can find unhealthy attachments to food and other substances. The relationship with your spouse that everyone expects to be strained and problematic is so often psychologically driven into the ground. In this reality, every single little thing in your daily co-parenting world has a layer of unnecessary difficulty and this gives a substantial amount of your time, over many years to come, to frustration, anger, and resentment. You'll easily put on hold all of your adventures of travel to places you've only dreamt of, your career advancement, the building of your artistic talents, and the music of your life which can simply be the mothering of your children, so that you may battle it out for control. This is the cost of divorce by typical standards. Everything you have built with your family – most importantly the quality of your relationships – in ruin. The fight for power and control will betray you and destroy everything, not to mention drain you financially, robbing you of what you value in life in your effort to rebuild.

Choose to follow me on this uncoupling journey to know in your heart what you need to do and feel certain about the choices you make along the way. You can go through this with a calm and optimistic mental state instead of letting the stress prematurely age you. You emerge from this looking and feeling your best, having honored your needs through the process. With this perspective, you will give yourself the upper hand in divorce negotiations and spend the very minimal amount of money for the best possible result. It will become possible to co-parent with cooperation and respect and you welcome the closeness with your children to become only more beautiful and intimate as they come into themselves. Should you give in to your desires in finding joy and personal transformation, you won't survive, you'll flourish. You get to blossom into the person you want to be and live a life you love. Instead of divorce stealing years from your life, it will bless you with more time spent in ways you've never experienced before, letting your spirit freely dance in ways that surpass your previous dabbling. Divorce is truly is what you make of it. If your marriage started beautifully, then it can transfigure with as much magnificence. You will be in the minority, and again and you will be less than understood. When you reach the other side of this uncoupling in your unusually auspicious way, people will deem you quite lucky. What they will not know is you made a specific choice, a commitment on the deepest level. It is this, not luck, that gives you the uniqueness of experiencing a loving divorce that opens the door to the prosperous future you made your reality.

CHAPTER 2

Where There Is a Will...

I met Ben when I was thirteen after having moved to a new school in eighth grade. He was in my science class. I have one memory of making an effort to talk to him when, for whatever reason, all the students were sent to the back of the classroom. He was quiet and looked interesting. His hair was to his shoulders, brown and wavy. I don't even remember what I had said. I was more outgoing than he. I think I remember him answering with a laugh. The conversation could have been comprised of two sentences. If you would have leaned over and whispered in my ear that we'd one day be married with three children, I would have slapped you in disbelief.

I made a friend that I passed the summer with and started my freshman year of high school in the fall. At lunch, I asked Ben's best friend to homecoming and he said yes. I really liked him. I'm not sure why. Mostly, I remember him being kind of quirky and cool, and I thought he was cute. He made some comment about how when he grew up, he'd make his kids eat vegetables, and that was it for me. We went out for maybe two months before he stood me up on a night I snuck out of the house. I never snuck out of the house, but this once, I did. I walked across town in the rain to meet him on the railroad tracks. I waited for maybe a half hour and walked home. I confronted him the next morning at school and he ignored me. By the end of the day, I had random people asking me about rumors I would deny, and recalling ugly stories they'd heard about me and my body. I deflated. As I was leaving to walk home at the end of the day, Ben approached me and apologized for his friend, comforting me. We sat on the front lawn of the school and talked for the first time, in this caring, intimate way. That's when I noticed how gorgeous his eyes were. That was the first spark, and the beginning of a relationship that lasted nearly twenty years.

High school was a time that I still consider one of the most difficult in my life. These were the years after my parent's divorce. Ben was the person who supported me through it. His family home was my refuge. His parents and siblings, their parties, their weekday family dinners and their holiday celebrations brought me a great deal of comfort and joy. When things at home were the hardest, and when my self-love was at an absolute low, Ben was there to love me. He also was hilariously witty and really artistically creative, which I particularly loved. Apparently, his long hair was indicative of being in a band, not doing drugs like I had originally assumed. In my last school there were drugs, not bands. He was incredibly talented on the drums and known at school for his artwork.

We were together seven and a half years before we were married at twenty-two. We had a beautiful, spirited wedding full of celebration. Everyone could feel the love between us. We had something unique. From there we started a spectacular life together. There were so many phenomenal aspects about it. We loved to travel and Ben edited together great family films. We sent out the craziest, funniest Christmas cards that went too far for conservative grandmothers and great-aunts. I had carefully built our relationship upon rules of respect and love that we abided by. We had managed to create something that was exceptionally honest and open.

Mixed somewhere in the middle of all this happiness were issues that went back to the very beginning of our relationship and followed us through to the end of our nineteen-year run together. The issue that took the cake? Sex. I'm not entirely sure when I began to dislike sex in my relationship. We were each other's firsts at an innocent age with a story that I look back on in a funny, sweet way. It was definitely consensual in the beginning, but by my wedding night, it had been years of me turning out the lights in hopes to just fall asleep, only it was very frequently not the case. For all sorts of reasons, I gave myself away in the bedroom to keep the peace. It seemed like an innocent fix for the moment, but in the background this pattern of behavior became a mounting issue. After about two years of marriage, I remember a phone call with Ben when I erupted with emotion, admitting I hated sex. "I would be happy never to have sex again for the rest of my life," I truthfully cried, telling him that I wished he'd have a mistress to take the burden off of me. I can't seem to put it into words how convoluted this subject was for me. All that I knew is that sex was a source of pain. It took me nine years after that conversation to uphold my personal boundaries and begin to understand what it was within our intimate dynamic that held us back.

As it turns out, our sexual issues were rooted within both of us, stemming from both of our families. At the time, I had placed full blame on myself. Even after I was able to identify my issues of taking my mother's childhood abuse as my own and doing the work to heal and move forward from it, he was unable to acknowledge the roots of his issues for the entirety of our marriage. We had five hundred conversations about our needs in this arena. I had been working so hard to unravel this mystery for myself *and* for him. Being in one relationship since childhood, it's incredibly difficult to tell exactly where one's issues end and their partner's begin. How would one have a sense of what's "normal" or how different it could be. For us, it proved impossible to discern. It has taken me being on the outside of my marriage and in a new relationship to have the perspective I needed to really make things clear, and I have learned so very much.

When I think about when we first started to struggle in our marriage, I think of two into the-night conversations on two separate vacations, both happening around the same time – about three years before I found myself sitting next to Ben in our dark bedroom for the late night talk that would end it for us. That period three years earlier was a time of great personal growth for me. It was right around the time that I had made some serious universe-trusting decisions, both with a financial risk. The first was to put my children in a Waldorf school, the second to employ an au pair from France to help me with my children so I could take on more hours at work to fund it all. After a altogether successful year, my beloved au pair returned to France and I was wrestling with feelings that wanted to send me into a different direction with work – I thought mostly of going back to school, but I couldn't figure out a way to make that possible financially nor timewise. I wanted to study linguistics, neuroscience, language, music theory, endocrinology, microbiology, dance, movement ... all the subjects that converge in my personal mini-verse that fuel me.

As the summer faded into the cold winter and as my questions of how I could satisfy this need in me became more pointed without resolution, my desperate heart was poised to break my daytime routine and find a call to action that would give me peace. The anxiety attacks caught me at random times with a sensation that drained all the blood from my head and sent me into a sharp downward spiral. These episodes did not let up and a dark time came over me. It was six months from the time they started to the point when finally had subsided. I was able to recognize this time in my life as what is commonly called a "dark night of the soul." And that it is, a dark fertile void, a sacred time of depression and deep personal growth, a sort of death and rebirth of oneself. As alone as one could feel going through it, it is a common experience in life. It is a response to an underlying current that connects us and fuels our vitality, creating profound shifts that can often and unexpectedly test the purpose of our partnerships.

The process through the pain was to reclaim myself, and to save my life. As I emerged from my dark night, I started to do the things I wanted to do. When Ben's interest lacked for my passions, I carved out a little time on my own, with an open invitation to join me. I had hoped he'd take interest. Afterall, this passion was *me.* Admittedly, I craved his support and encouragement, and just deep to this, his approval and admiration for my own creative nature. I had begun the adventure in finding this for myself. I started to sew, read poetry and do Pilates. I would skip out on things I usually did with him that I didn't love, like watching TV shows every night before bed. Having different interests proved inconsequential for the most part. More significant was that I started being intimate with him on my own terms. This meant respecting my feelings and giving myself the right to say what I wanted and what I did not want, whenever it should come up.

It was in this time period I would remark to Ben that my future seemed to be turning to white. It was an intuition, I suppose. Perhaps because I was taking control of my life and shaping my destiny in ways I could not yet imagine, the projector in my mind started to fade out on the white canvas. It's worth noting that this started to happen simultaneously with the filling in of *me* into my life. I was connecting with my very own path. I had always the impulse to live life to the fullest and now I found myself committed to my highest purpose in this world, whatever I should discover of it.

I'll never forget the day that I had a momentary vivid mental image of seeing *the white* headed down my street toward my house. I asked myself, "What will happen when it arrives?" And then one day, it did. All was white. And I just stared into it. It lasted days, maybe weeks. By this time, I had made a nice dent in becoming my new, confident self, and somehow my marriage had ended, my home was to be sold, the children's time at the Waldorf school had ended, and nothing in my future was in view. When homelife ended with my high school sweetheart, I had not an inkling of where I was to go next. I had lost completely my identity, yet I had never been so sure of who I was.

To help me navigate this nebulous time, I did a lot of things:

I listened to guided meditation every night for the first four months straight after I was separated. This grounded me. I liked the ones where I got to meet my future self. Before bed, these guided meditations deeply relaxed me and brought me back to center, back into my body and into a deep and relaxing sleep. It was hugely important for my well-being.

I would meditate on my own. I would tune into my body and pay attention to sensations that I would feel. And while I did this, I would record myself as I talked aloud and described every detail about what the sensations felt like, looked like, and how they changed while I focused on them. This is a technique I use with my clients adapted from my years of being a craniosacral therapist and clairsentient. It is a way to let go of physical pain and discomfort that arises during a stressful time by connecting sensation with emotions, experiences, and memories that surface in the words of our descriptions. It is through our bodies' language of sensation that acts as a portal into our deepest selves, allowing us to open further in meeting our own needs.

I talked to God, to angels, to guides, to my deceased great-grandparents, to fairies, animal spirits, to the moon, to whoever or whatever came through as a force I felt was guiding me though at that moment.

I paid attention to my dreams and would write them down or record them. This gave me a lot of insight into the situations I was facing, how I was handling them and what lay ahead.

I made audio notes daily about what I was going through, how I was stuck or sad or angry, and would listen to my own recordings in order to process them more thoroughly and gain perspective. This truly saved me. There is something that changes the game when you hit record. It's like someone is listening. There's only so much talking to the people around you that you can do, for their sake and yours. You are the keeper of your own answers. Why not talk to yourself? Talking aloud really helps you to process your thoughts. When the words stay inside your head, they remain unchanged to a great degree. When you say a thought out loud, your body responds to it the same way as if someone else had said it. It's funny. I see it all the time in my dialog work with clients. There's a huge shift in a body when you vocalize something. It becomes exposed and workable.

I also had two friends I could talk to who were broad-minded, asking me questions that would allow me to interrupt my own patterns of belief. It's fantastic if you have someone in your life you can open up to in this way. Both women were going through separations of their own, one of which had already initiated a diffi-cult divorce from her husband, and my other dear con-fidant, was going through her own version of my story. Having shut down intimately, she was unfulfilled in her daytime role, and was desperate to quell the compul-sion to set off for the sunset bound for freedom to live out her truth- as I imagined it, her unexpressed wild child would have touched down in the Amazon, soul seeking without parameters. She did not make a run for it, however. Instead she spoke this truth explicitly to her husband, and to my fascination, after setting her boundaries and expressing her needs, her husband said he would support her to do anything she needed to, kicked into high gear with all the daytime domestic duties and demanded she not give up on him. He made a conscious effort to do everything he could to make it into the next chapter of life together. Mind blowing, I thought. That had not been the response I got. And then I watched her face the very different and difficult challenge to find the strength and desire to reinvest herself in her relationship. She got what she asked for, only after she had emotionally detached. In so many ways, her situation seemed harder than mine, yet I find envy in their ability to stay together. These companions brought so much enlightenment and comfort to my experience. They were my right-hand women, and carried me through a crucial time. Who you choose to share this time with is influential to your well-being. Your companions should pick you up, hold you accountable, let you dream and make you think. Allow yourself to spend time only with those to whom you can bare your soul and leave their presence with a feeling of renewal. Let us always remember to show them our gratitude.

It is important you feel fully supported by others along with your stellar independent work. Do have someone around you that broadens the landscape of your thinking or perhaps you can buy the services of a few helpers? Do you see someone for bodywork, or talk to a therapist or coach? Are you interested in crystal healing or joining a meditation group? Surround yourself with the kind of energy you want to generate. Immersion is key. Build a team and don't be afraid to invest in yourself. If you have to step outside your immediate circle to find support, consider it a sign that it is now the time to welcome the arrival of new people into your life. Start by simply by tuning into uplifting music, chanting and listening to motivational speakers while you get ready in the morning, are in the car, and as you fall asleep. Surround yourself with positivity.

How did I move on from my marriage when I had been with him my whole life? With care, with certainty and with a lot of support. This guide serves to be a companion in finding your own true answers you can trust, giving you the tools, perspective, and confidence to know how you want to move forward and live your life, starting today.

CHAPTER 3

Your Survival Guide

This book is more than a survival guide. It's your thrive guide. It's designed to take you from whatever situation you are in now, to living out your best-case scenario. It enables you to go through the process of divorce while maintaining a working relationship with your ex, negotiating a fair agreement, and being an attentive parent by letting you in on the secrets of how to be unusually successful in experiencing a kind and generous uncoupling. In order to do that we'll be journaling the answers to lots of questions as well as meditating and visualizing as we go, so if you don't have a journal, I would suggest investing in a special one.

The writing itself is pretty light-hearted and optimistic, but it's not because I don't know what you are going through. With a transition of this magnitude, you don't thrive without first having to face some truly difficult emotions. As you flow through it, you'll notice that sometimes you're down and sometimes you're up. There is a good reason for this and you shouldn't put pressure on yourself to be happy all the time or to have all the answers. There is biological rhythm throughout this process that leads us through pockets of emotions as part of our healing. It is a current that you can trust and every time you feel your head dip under the surface of your emotions, you will eventually and naturally rise back up for air – I promise you. Use the time when submerged in emotion explore further into the rabbit hole. Each time you go in, you will be invited to connect with particular emotions, beliefs, and memories, many of which will have a component hidden to you, a falsehood woven in, hence the misery. The overarching principal being: Truth feels good. Falsity feels bad. You will want to journal your exploration either by writing or speaking into a voice recorder. You will certainly learn something of value as you come back up to the surface. Should you desire further insight, reviewing your notes in a better state of mind can help you see the bigger picture, validate your concerns, open new ideas and like a forensic investigator, carefully pluck the fibers of your own pessimistic fiction from your thought process.

This book is designed to transport you out of your daily stresses so that you can gain perspective and find clarity when you return to your day-to-day. As you can imagine, your world looks very differently depending on what mind frame you're in and what you're focusing on. This book is inviting you into different mind spaces. It's meant to be easy and playful and engage your imagination. Chapters will often include breaks for visualizations, meditations, and questions to ponder. Take your time as you read to process along with me. You will get so much more from reading if you move into the exploratory parts of it. So, don't bother to count down the chapters or pages. I wanted this book to be as short and sweet as it is profound and lovingly helpful. In order to get the most from this guide, you must allow yourself to be present and follow yourself into your emotions exploring them as much as possible. I'll give you a hundred ways you can do that.

I tend not to take religious or spiritual views at face value. I perceive the truths of the universe to be too broad for my small human brain to accurately conceptualize. Rather, I trust the broader element of myself to feel this truth and leave open my gaps of knowledge willingly. Not only are we limited in our concepts of the universe, we are a thousand more times limited in our language and how we can express our experiences of the universe. Having a deep respect for religion and philosophy, my language reflects the vocabulary from every ideology I've explored. With all my senses, I note the gut feelings of truth in phenomena around me, in the healing work I facilitate, in stories shared by others and within religious and spiritual teachings. With regards to lingual limitations, I choose the words that are the closest match in meaning. I would be unable to tell you I believe in reincarnation for example, and yet I use this word as I believe in the phenomena that is best described as reincarnation. I consider the idea that reincarnation may be more abstract than it is traditionally understood, and, therefore, lovingly limited to make sense to human minds.

Similarly, when you speak to your children with complete honesty about your separation and divorce with the whys and hows, you're going to have to put it in words they understand, since communication — the comprehension of the information — is what matters most. So, it is between the heavens and this world I believe the grand truth becomes a loving, slightly simplified version, so that humanity can grasp the concept and use the knowledge to benefit us. Along the same lines, when I use the word God, I could just as easily use the words source, the collective, the universe, Great Spirit, and so on. For a time, I avoided using the word God, but as of late, I have gotten used to it again. The people I have been chatting with speak of God as something more expansive and loving than the identically named, somewhat severe personage I had previously moved away from. I speak the languages of spirituality interchangeably and find the translations interesting. My writing will likely reflect that I am always tuned into the guiding forces of nature, of the cosmos, and all the energies that come through as angels, fairies, ancestral spirits, animal guides, and beyond. I don't discriminate. I derive a special joy in feeling the presence of our guides and welcome you to deeply connect with the energies that surround, comfort and guide you through your journey. There will also be reference to terminology and practices, like co-dependence, twin flames, affirmations, law of attraction, self-hypnosis, meditation and the like. I am not going to go into depth about these subjects since they are rather well-established and taught by others, but if you find yourself unsure about what they are and how to do them, I recommend doing a little research and diving in simultaneously along with this guide, especially if you identify with the concept.

This uncoupling book journey starts with the moment when divorce is put squarely on the table and your whole life flashes in front of your eyes. From the moment you separate, there's a whole bunch of unraveling that has to be done, that happens *for* you. From here, life is carefully dismantled and so, a rebuilding commences. If you are able to be conscious throughout, you'll have much more success in getting your needs met in this very volatile phase. You can champion this time with a sense of stability, feeling more or less in control, instead of the typical method of losing one's mind, raging and prematurely aging or eating and drinking your way through it. Hold tight and follow me through this and you can keep your hair and good looks and make it to the other side with flying colors. When you feel good, life is good. And if you are conscious in your rebuilding of your life, which literally happens as you dismantle, you can make choices that make you happy rather than allow life to happen to you. You can try your hand at designing this new beginning, making it different in ways that could potentially delight you. Not to mention you may have multiple little ones to care for and maintaining a solid connection to the ground is paramount for them. Included are some important things I learned along the way about how children process divorce and how to recognize particular behaviors and respond to them. It surprised me to see this unusual acting out firsthand and I see a lot of parents that misinterpret their children's behaviors. Also included is a chapter that runs down what to expect legally and how this divorce thing works. When someone says, "I'm leaving," neither person really knows what all is involved besides the fact that you're breaking up. It will be nice to have a sense of what has to happen to make it legal and official which, I'll tell you now, feels much like a pregnancy – by month ten, you're feeling very tired and ready for relief.

My goal in this book is to guide you through a peaceful separation and divorce process, a conscious uncoupling book designed specifically for women who have been with their partner since childhood and who haven't experienced adult life without being with the other. There are lots of hilariously frightening moments, like losing your second virginity, that have some extra layers of scary that no one else will understand. I want to be able to share with you some stories as we go with the intentions bonding and making room for processing your own experiences. If a book could be a two-way conversation, I'd want this to be it. I'm a therapist, and a really good friend, and I love to open up space for your memories, thoughts, dreams, ideas ... for your energy, a sort of shared diary of comradery, of wisdom and deep expression.

By the end, we should be able to reflect with gratitude on how far we came. We should be able to look at the people that shared in our journey for the better or worse and know what fruit of knowledge they offered us and our delight that we now have this abundance of wisdom and self-assurance in our life. You'll be ready, new diary in hand, to embark on the next chapter of your story, prepared for all the adventures you choose and ready to seize the day!

CHAPTER 4

How You Got Here, and What That Means for You

*"Here is life, an experiment to a great
extent untried by me; but it does not
avail me that [my seniors] have tried it.
If I have any experience which I think
valuable, I am sure to reflect that this
my Mentors said nothing about."*

– Henry David Thoreau, Walden

When we start this journey, this labyrinth, we know not what is before us. Life takes shape around us. The ground gathers at our feet. Our mothers and fathers come out to meet us and we take the plunge, pushing our bodies forward though a rite of passage into this world and into our lives. Each person around us helps form us. Each experience opens our horizons to see ourselves beyond where we stand. Your life has come together just so.

With all of these powers and influences, from within to the world outside you, and from the outside world in, your life has taken shape.

Stand with me inside of Stonehenge for a moment. Stop and breathe and take it in. You can see on all sides of you the horizon. You see the sun appearing in the sky ahead. You feel your ancestors in this place before you. You feel them in the ground and in the slabs of cold rock. You imagine the people of this place six thousand years before, traveling from one end of the earth to the other. Imagine what forces took them there. And imagine that *because* they built this circle temple right here, six millennia ago, you are standing right here, right now.

Many moons ago, people who came before you made decisions that brought you to where you grew up, and to where you possibly still live in this world. You speak the language you speak because nations took over other nations, because groups of people migrated and mixed with other people. How much of your life is the way it is now because of choices ancestors made thousands of years ago? Much. And as we draw the timeline in nearer and closer to our own arrival onto this earth we can see how our great grandparents, our grandparents, and our parents did things that shaped our lives, our beliefs and our personalities. This concept is one I call lineage. It does exist in the genetic information passed down as well as the habits and beliefs, one might say, the environmental factors that we pass down through generations, but I will take it one step further and suggest that there is yet another way that information is passed down to us, and that is by energetic imprint. It is uncanny how our stories can resemble those of the people that came before us. Part of our mission here is all about tying up loose ends by healing and overcoming our challenges. Yet let us not get bogged down in adversity. We also carry through energetic imprints to further great works, talents and gifts. Whatever you discover you have brought through from the generations before you, you are most certainly trailblazing. A tremendous amount of peace may be found when we honor the work in this realm, conscious or unconscious. It is an advantage to have the ability to be aware of it. It provides a stable underlying framework for gratitude for those that allow us to wrestle, problem solve and flex our muscles. In moments like this one, when literally everything in your life is shifting, we see lines of lineage light up like a firework display offering a tremendous shift in expression, story and emotion, a celebration of an emergence and a finale of a hundred elements coming full circle, synapses firing, and lots of oohs and ah-has.

Working to Heal Lineage

I had a great-grandfather whose name wasn't allowed to be said in my home growing up. He was a family

35

offender, having abused my mother and my aunt when they were quite young. I learned about this when I was rather young and I had two personal responses to it. The first was to try and help my wounded mother to heal from this and move on. I later wondered if I found my life's work as a healer and therapist because of this beginning. The second response was a fear that I could have somehow been the dreaded Pappi reincarnated. He was a monster that I didn't want to ever identify with, and so naturally I did out of fear. As a young person, I didn't have a concept of sexuality, and couldn't comb out what was perverse, so I encapsulated it all together and distanced myself. I had essentially grown up feeling myself a victim of abuse, without experiencing it first-hand. And I did what abused people often do; I found myself in a relationship where I could wrestle with feeling like a victim. I contended with a disconnected energy within my intimate relationship, and at times an insensitivity to my feelings and desires. I was unconsciously perpetuating this pattern into my own life. Why would I do this? Why would anyone take on energetic baggage in the first place? I'd like to suppose that we feel up to the challenge on some level, and that it is in service that we heal these ancestral lines, and thus, the world through our collective consciousness.

In healing this lineage, we allow ourselves to fully move on, no longer subject to the energetic tugs that trigger us to be pulled out of alignment and into the funky dynamics that we get ourselves in. When we break through, it sends a wave down an entire line of people that came before you, releasing tensions that exist from within and flow outward. You heal not just yourself but a constellation of ancestors.

What did your parents go through that you feel echoed in your life? What did your husband bring into the relationship from his parents? And from grands and great-grands?

One night, after a strained intimate moment I had with my husband, I found myself again groping around for answers and fell into despair, sobbing and retreating to the backyard with the decision that I would grin and bear it. I would depend on my strength and willpower to climb the mountain on my own, I thought. I would solve the problems of my marriage for both myself and my husband ... and at that idea, I wailed with sadness and saw a vision of my mother, of her mother, and of her mother before that. I knew in that moment I was following the footsteps of the women before me. That's when I retracted my choice to muscle through the problem myself. I took a deep inhale of dark cold spring air. I remember the scent of wet, decayed leaves from last fall. It was such a dark night. I could hardly see anything at all. Perhaps that's why the glowing faces of my mito-chondrial mothers seemed to burn their images into my retinas. I went back in the house.

How to Recognize What Patterns Contributed to Your Current Situation

There is so much of trauma that gets carried on through the generations. Not just trauma, but shame, limiting beliefs, and negative self-talk that is taken on. This energy shapes us. It shapes our decisions that then shape our relationships and our experiences. Take a moment now to reflect on these influences in your life. Grab your notebook for this chapter. We'll explore the dynamic you feel between you and your husband and how much of this comes from unresolved lineage.

So, what do we do with this baggage? Well, it's a lot easier to do something with it when we know it isn't ours. It is as simple as we make it. Just ... let ... go. It doesn't belong to you. It's like walking down the street and realizing you've got bags in your hands, perhaps one strapped to your back, and you can just put them down and walk away. Or, if you have a flare for the dramatic and would like to let go of some extra emotion while you are at it, you could imagine throwing your baggage into a lake, or into a volcano. You could magically transform the bag into something else ... your imagination is key to know what is the best way to let go or how to transmute this energy. Your imagination is a secret agent of intuition. It's limitless. When we use imagination as a tool, we can let go of all rules and work that much closer to our truth.

So, if it is so easy to let go of the baggage, why are we often unable to do it? In one word, *attachment*. We are attached to it, addicted to it. And that seems so crazy because we don't want it. It's not easy to see how this drain on your life actually serves you in some way, even if it's serving you on a very low level. Have you ever tried to shut down your computer and there's an error because there's a program still running? You have to cancel out of everything, open the program that's running so that you can close it out, and recommence shut down. When you try to let go of family lineage, and you just can't seem to leave it behind you, it's because your program is still running. That's why you can't just let it go. You use it.

I'll give you a nice example of mine. I can be overly critical of myself and not even realize it. I just assume that my work is a bit worse than it is. "No, you don't get it," I'd say. "It's not good, really." The funny thing is that it doesn't even feel like I'm being critical; just realistic. Then I caught myself being truly blind to my worth and merit, and I knew I had to change it. Now, where did this pattern come from? I know it's from childhood, but when? Was I born this way? I can tell you that my mother has the same issue. Most of the time when I negatively critique myself, there's no tangible consequence. It's just a bummer. But every once in a while, when I truly need the confidence that I can accomplish something, that pattern of thinking will take me down. Especially if it's a moment when I am seeking performance. When I'm stopped from progressing with crappy self-criticism, I want like hell to chuck it out the window because it makes me terribly upset. Only this is what happens: I run up to the open, second-floor window of an office building with my old-fashioned camel leather brief case filled with limited self-worth. I wind up, rapidly approach the opening, go to hurl it out into the open air — and my fingers don't unclasp, my fist holds tight to the handle and I spin around in a circle and lose my balance toward the floor. What the hell? Why can't I let go? "Oh, well it turns out," A snobbish inner voice says in a moment of introspection, "I use criticism to keep me down." Why would I do that? "Oh, well," the assuring voice continues, "I need to keep myself from doing my best work in case that it sucks... You know, because it feels like I'm going to die when I'm embarrassed. *If* by chance I *am* delusional in thinking my work is good, unaware that the rest of the world actually finds it subpar, I'll die of humiliation." And then my little fingers that had just sabotaged my release of that old briefcase of self-doubt, straighten out their shirts and waistcoats to be recognized as victoriously preserving me. I tried to shut down my program, all the while using it. I tried to release my oppressive beliefs but my subconscious said, "Nope. I need that." Of course, this is not the end of the story. There *is* a way to chuck your limiting beliefs and old destructive patterns and create fantastic, new useful ones.

If you tried to drop your briefcase only to find it stick to your hand, answer this very important question: How does it benefit me to keep it? How are you using this low level programming installed by previous generations to keep you safe? By identifying your fears and shedding light on them, updating your programming with a new perspective, you can try again to let go and move on. With those big, nicely engrained patterns, you might stand at that second-floor window with faulty finger-opening twenty times. If this is the case, don't let this disappoint you. I'll let you in on a secret that will make your twentieth try worth it: you are chipping away at what is nearing a personal gold mine. The more entrenched this old patterning is for you, the more it's been interrupting your mojo. The more wrapped up this programming is in your life and work it takes to release it, the more likely it is *the key* to your success. And not just a little success, a really huge transformation that has potential to release the biggest emotional blockage of your life, followed by unpresented richness. Every day that you whittle away will give you positive results along the way. The work adds up faster than you think, and the unprecedented fulfillment and joy that you are able to experience because you stuck with it makes it all sublimely worth it.

There is a mini-step that happens immediately after we sever cords to the past that is worth mentioning. This is to give yourself a moment to tune into yourself to heal any wound left behind from severing this previous attachment. This can be done with visualization, or using your own hands to channel warmth and love to the part of your body that feels affected. It's a simple honoring of oneself and the closing of a channel. It is sealed with love and gratitude.

Finally, we get to the part where you engineer a new behavior of your own design, based on *your* energy and *your* beliefs and patiently integrating it into every part of your life, in every relationship and situation. You do this by simply consciously practicing your chosen behavior in real life. In my case, I started correcting self-criticism immediately with encouragement, a choice to open myself to positive feedback and compliments. And my newest favorite affirming habit is tattooing "I am better than I think" on my forehead by writing it letter by letter with my finger. It's been a quite helpful reminder.

It's important to note that you can expect yourself to go into your old patterns sometimes. Don't be distracted with disappointment. Afterall, how can you expect a new river to flow a contrary route atop a canyon bed of well-worn in thinking? It takes time and perseverance. Not a million years, but a lot of work the first month. You will be prepared shift perception and implement your new behavior. This is a golden opportunity to respond in a way that is true to who we are at our core, and throw off the heavy robe of our predecessors.

Your Lineage and Where You Stand Today

So what gems of knowledge do we get out of pondering our lineage and how it contributes to where you are today? While we've been examining lineage as the deconstructing of old patterns, surprisingly enough you will likely find lineage in your new chosen patterns. Your trailblazing might just remind you of the people that came before you as well. When I found myself in a position to write my first book, wouldn't you know that I had unintentionally followed my grandmother in being an author- my spiritual grandma that speaks french, sings and taught me energy healing. It would seem I carry forward many of the talents she has lovingly cultivated. Many of my other interests also have surprised me having discovered family from generations earlier having developed skills I have and still desire. What interests do you have in mind to pursue? What is your preferred lifestyle?

When we reflect on our marriage, we can briefly look at what bonded you together.

What did you overcome together?

What are you leaving this relationship with now that you didn't have before you met?

What baggage had you brought into the relationship that you had successfully moved beyond?

And one should spend a moment to consider what happened in the eleventh hour of your relationship that brought you to this moment. Here are a few questions meant to shed some light for your reflection:

What shift took place that put strain on the area of your relationship that caused it to break? What are the reasons behind your separation?

What are you not willing to give up in this transition?

How did you feel most limited in your relationship?

What is most pressing on your mind as it currently stands?

After you've journaled the answers to these questions, you will see in front of your eyes the reason why you stand in this moment with clarity. You stand in a place of great power. You mustn't forget it.

What does your position of power invite you to do?

CHAPTER 5

The Catalyst

There had been a particularly blustery day before my separation, where the clouds swirled a dark grey meringue. I was driving down the street, right down from my house. As my windshield wipers flipped back and forth in the downpour, one of my windshield wipers flew straight off my car. I yelped in astonishment. I pulled over the car and picked up my wiper, and as I walked back around the front of my car something stopped me. I looked up at the sky. I turned my head instinctively to the left. The winds had shifted. Something was coming, I knew. I was still for another moment and returned to my seat in the car. I saw it coming. I felt it. It's interesting how one can feel the actual change of course in one's life with the way a wind can cut across you. And for me, the breakthrough was quite literal, and would come straight for us barreling down the same street.

At some specific point in my journey, I started to veer away from my old patterns. I felt compelled to answer my heart and venture into self-discovery. Did you adventure begin similarly? Unknowingly then that you would find yourself here, facing divorce. Your uncoupling is part of a bigger loop with a conclusion that circles back to the beginning, in this case, to your self-discovery and self-expression. This joy in feeling like yourself again will motivate you and magnetically pull you forward. What does your future have in store for you? We can get a strong sense by looking at the significant things that had a hand in calling it quits.

What was the catalyst that ended your relationship? You may identify a few things that put you in the position to divorce, but what stands out at the most influential? This is the fascinating conversation of this chapter. It is this subject matter that I had nearly decided to make the entire focus of my book.

It's worth telling you right away that I will be guiding you to find your own answers rather than feed you generalities. Nothing about your experience with your catalyst is general. It is very specific to you, and with that I have reverence and fascination in the discoveries of your truth through this. In all my years of work, I know that it is in listening, not thinking, that we find authenticity. And it shall be through the sharing of enlightenment that we walk together, our torches to light the path. The world the catalyst presents to you is a crazy adventure to say the least. A rollercoaster ride of exhilaration, heart-wrenching sadness, bliss, fear, and peace. Was it all worth it?

I will share how the high price of this experience, when recognized, becomes unmeasurable in value. What is the purpose of the catalyst and how do we attach false importance to them? After you've identified what your catalyst is, we will talk about what the next steps are in handling it. How do you get the most out of this experience? What do you do if your feelings are still unresolved? I will make a special note regarding twin flames should this be how your catalyst presented itself, talk about the real reason why you're getting divorced, and why it matters that you make the distinction between the real reason and the catalyst. I will illuminate my torch of understanding of how the choice one makes in this facet of your uncoupling can either bring you peaceful resolution and a positive new beginning, or the non-choice that continues your rollercoaster experience well past the point where you are ready to get off the ride.

There's usually someone or something that happens that has a really big role in making marital issues come to a head. It's the game changer, a needed element that shook things up a bit and made an issue impossible to ignore. This is your catalyst. There can be a few elements that ratcheted things up for you, but the catalyst is special in the way that the whole divorce could be blamed on it. It is so powerful, that your entire understanding of the situation was eventually blown open with blatant awakening. Marital discussions are pushed into overdrive. Without it, it is possible that issues could have continued to bubble up in your relationship, the resolution still waiting to fully come to fruition.

Besides the critical role the catalyst plays in you finally dealing with the most desperate issue in your marriage, the actual experience of it is really complex and interesting. There's a good chance that when this energy enters your life, it creates a world of its own for a while. So, if we want to be able to move forward in our lives, we have to also have a good understanding of our catalyst, why it affected us the way it did, and what we want to do with it.

The Ratcheting

There were a lot of things that happened in the years leading up to my divorce that had a profound impact. My six month dark night of the soul was probably the thing that sent my relationship in a new direction. As painful as that was, it was responsible for being able to identify my needs and take them seriously. I was confronted with the deeply unsettling feeling of dying if I didn't grow. I needed to change my life's work and my path. I had untouched interests and potential that would no longer stay hidden in the dark depths of my being.

48

Two months before my relationship was to end, another significant notch happened right before Thanksgiving. It was but a month after my windshield wiper flew off my car and I had stepped outside to witness the wind change direction in my life. I had entertained a small family dinner party that evening. That night after cleaning up, I lay down to rest on the daybed in the front room of my home. I was just drifting to sleep when Ben asked if I wanted to come upstairs to bed, and in that moment, I opened my eyes and stared at a small digital clock in my line of sight. I debated if I'd like to snooze there or head up right away. When I think back to that moment, I see angels hoisting me onto my feet to head up. An hour later, there was a tremendous blast. The sound of broken glass echoed in my ears. I got out of bed and walked down the stairs to see through the front of my home. I could see my street through a gigantic hole in the wall. I stepped though the shattered glass and shards of furniture, the daybed partially smashed and pushed into the middle of the room. It was like a bomb had gone off. As I walked barefoot into the deafeningly silence of mid-night onto the icy pavement of my front walkway, I looked down my driveway and there lay a car, flipped completely upside down, half resting atop one of our cars and smashed into the other, with a young woman trapped inside.

I yelled into the exposed family room for Ben to call an ambulance and proceeded down the cold, debris

49

laden driveway towards the wreckage. I heard a small voice from inside fearfully cry for help. I answered her, soothing her that help was on the way and that I was here. I tried to open the upside down passenger side door that faced me. It was locked. So I crouched and moved behind the back of the car that had been lifted and resting on my other car, found the hollow of the smashed drivers side window and crawled in to find her. It was so disorienting inside. I put my hand on her belly, her torso exposed as she was in fact upside down, her legs off to the side, the steering while pinned to her chest- her upper body lost and out of sight under the crumpled front end of her car. There was no possible way for her to budge. I calmly spoke and assured her, with a motherly caress to her belly, as the poor sweet girl's head was trapped and confined, out of sight for me to know for certain if she were to survive. I thought of her mother, heart breaking just to experience her nightmare. When help arrived, they made me move away. When my dear neighbor arrived, I threw myself in his arms and sobbed. I waited for forty-five minutes as they cut the car apart to extract her. To my utter relief, she was conscious and whole. After my home was boarded up, I left the scene with my family and stayed with my mother. It took courage to come back the next day. Would it be worse or better than we expected? As we reentered the destruction, morale sank. What devastation... Our home, our heirlooms, both cars totaled, cabinetry meant for the kitchen in our garage smashed by my car pushed through the garage door, five insurance claims and insufficient credit to buy a new car. Days later, I saw in the news that she had only suffered a minor ankle injury. To my disappointment, she had been driving while intoxicated.

This pivotal moment is one that many people assumed was the catalyst in our divorce.

Those people included our oldest daughter, who will forever see that fateful strike to house and home having changed the trajectory of our family forever. She's not wrong to believe that. The house getting smashed did put us in a rather precarious situation. It certainly changed the circumstances around our finances so drastically that it allowed us to sell the house that we mortgaged for more than it was valued for over decade. It transformed our belongings into cash that would facilitate the start of separate lives. It played a very significant role in allowing us to make what otherwise would have been a logistically impossible transition. It felt as if the house were struck personally by the hand of God. It was undeniable in its emotional impact on everyone in our family. And yet, it was not the catalyst in our divorce. Without it, I may not have found myself sitting on that bed, taking in Ben's final decision he'd had enough. And yet, it was never brought up in conversation on that late night. It was nowhere on our minds.

The Catalyst

Our catalyst came in the form of a French teacher. The story begins while driving by myself across Ohio, recording my thoughts on my voice recorder. In my effort to put more time and energy in nurturing my own growth and meeting my own needs, I made a list of all the things I wanted to accomplish that would make me feel great. The first thing on my list to do? Speak French fluently. This was the first and the most important personal goal I had ever made for myself since childhood. French was the last living language in my family. My grandparents spoke fluently. Without having met this goal, I felt I was undoubtedly failing myself. Speaking French was breathing in life. At this point I still couldn't hold a conversation. Finances in my marriage were always a bit of a strain, and it was hard for me to find money for my interests. On my sunny ride home though Ohio, I decided, money or not, I would return to language learning. And as the sun dropped toward the horizon, I caught sight of a cloud so beautiful with the sun positioned directly behind it, that its silver lining was set aflame. I pulled over to take a picture. After arriving home, I called a teacher that had advertised on a neighborhood restaurant window, here in my small town looking for language students!

It turned out by the time I called him, he no longer lived in my town. He was living about a half hour away, taking care of his newborn baby, just about to move to Ohio. He agreed to Skype lessons. What happened next was completely unexpected and consciously unsolicited. Suffice to say, I learned more French in our six months of classes than I had ever learned in my life. But I also had my very first experience of being knocked off my feet by this endlessly invigorating emotion that felt a lot like being uncontrollably in love. It was weird. It was *really* weird. Maybe it was my relative disinterest in sex for my entire life until that point, but I'm telling you, I was hit from left field, totally bemused by the whole situation, and eventually completely astounded that I could have a really sexy passionate side waiting to get out. It was the greatest news in the world because until then, my only solution to lack of vitality in my sex life had been to discuss and pain endlessly with my husband, question my libido, and buy supplements. I took this newfound information straight to my husband. Of course, right? That's what anyone would do.... I'm going to guess that this aspect of my relationship was unique. I don't bother hiding feelings. It sounds like a lot of effort to me. I held space for true, unfiltered honesty delivered in love and consideration. The result of this openness between Ben and I, allowed us to connect in ways we never had before. It did bring a spark to the bedroom for us, though the core of our intimacy problems was much deeper than either one of us could get a grasp on when we were together, and ultimately it did not fix our problem.

Interestingly enough, Ben understood the connection I felt with my tutor, wanting to also experience this kind of connection with someone for himself. He ended up meeting someone online soon after, exploring this interest long distance. Some of my favorite memories were of cracking open a fancy beer after dinner and talking about these people in our lives, usually about how crazy the girl he was talking to was. It was funny and interesting, and seriously amusing. I could see Ben as a separate person than I, which was really engaging. We felt rather safe because neither pseudo relationship was in person. The fact that this was nourishing rather than detrimental speaks to our experience being high school sweethearts, never having another experience with which to compare anything. Getting to see a glimpse of who Ben was without me was so interesting to me. And I started to see what I brought to the table.

I knew from the beginning, in my heart of hearts, that even though my connection with my French teacher was very real and very special in a soulful way, it was something I had to let go of. I think this made the brush with a twin flame easier for me, though the fact it was very unrealistic we could ever be together felt like being worse off. It felt like bumping into your soulmate only to be told, "No, not this life." I experienced this in a kind of protective bubble, unlike others who experience being face-to-face with a kind of chemistry that turns a spark into an uncontrollable blaze. This I can easily under-

54

stand happening in others' stories, and should there be a possibility of being together and starting a relationship, I can imagine how difficult of a situation that would be. It was the first time I felt anything like obsession, just because I daydreamt every single day for a year about him. It was an intense feeling of love, excitement, sensuality, sadness, insecurity, and loss. By the end, I was waiting for the moment my mind would release him. I asked the universe to be able to let go forever, and eventually a distinguishable moment arrived when I realized with emotion, there was in fact a world outside of my catalyst. What a relief.

The saving grace in having ventured into the world of the catalyst was that I did so very consciously. It's a powerful experience that has the potential to ignite the kind of change needed in your relationship and overcome a profound issue together, making you stronger and closer than ever. I had fallen head over heels for someone else, but I was aware enough to ask the universe what this was all about, and courageous enough to listen for an answer. Through my honesty with Ben, we were able to explore for ourselves. He comforted me when I cried in letting go of this twin flame person of mine, but interestingly enough, after I had decided to end all conversation with my French teacher for good, Ben encouraged me to reach back out to my teacher romantically, as an effort to revive my spark. Of course, I did not reach out. But, this was a powerful message for me moving forward, one that helped me keep my wits about me in the end, because it was my French teacher that took center stage in that dark room's one-way conversation. I was blamed for having feelings for another, and this was his reason to leave me. It was over. Darkness. Stillness. I took some unfair blows, but with respect and listening with my heart rather than my head. What he had said was true. But it wasn't the reason he was leaving.

What I understood about my twin flame was that he allowed me to connect deeply with myself. He brought out something in me I hadn't known existed. It was something really powerful that seemed to tap into the very core of my strength, and manifested for me in many ways. It expressed itself with getting into the best shape of my life with athletics and it had a strength of voice in going after the things I desired in life. It felt no shame, it loved its wild sexuality, seeing it as the divine feminine and oh how she was glorious. I wanted to explore and expand upon this energy in me. This energy belonged to me, not my catalyst, and I wasn't about to let it go when I let him go. My silver lining set ablaze, and it was just the beginning.

The Real Reason

The real reason my marriage ended was because of an emptiness that existed in my dear childhood sweetheart, that I couldn't fill or make complete. When I stopped trying to satiate this need in him, this inner void desperately searched for another source in someone else. This is the undercurrent showing itself once again. This time, carrying Ben below the water into the icy depths. Its purpose is higher. And it was with love that I let go. I knew that I couldn't provide what he was searching for that would ultimately bring him into the beauty of wholeness. Isn't that what love is about, having the other's best interest at heart, no matter what? If we can discern between the socially unacceptable and blamable catalyst and the real reason for the divorce being a true need for something that the marriage won't support, this changes the playing field completely. It will allow you to keep your conversations on point, speaking only to what truly matters. It pacifies anger and resentment and it gives you the grace of letting go with the opportunity to ask yourself this question, "How can I love even more?"

Because I understood the purpose behind my twin flame, I could put it in perspective. I'm very aware that this is a very difficult thing to do, because the pleasure is so intense. But the pain, it's equally tremendously awful. And the truth was that within my situation, one didn't exist without the other. I choose not a mixture of pleasure and pain, truth and fallacy, real and illusionary, spirit and ego. I want to stand in truth – the elemental light – it's serene; it's joy. Good feelings grow out of truth as it resonates with your heart, bad feeling are diseased with falsehood. It's easy to identify them if they're on their own. It gets confusing when you mix those energies together. I couldn't choose a relationship that creates good-bad feelings. I prefer to take all of the amazing feelings, that belong to me anyway, forward with me.

So, it should be said that your feelings belong to you. They're all yours. Your love belongs to you and only you. It's your feeling. If someone loves you, it's theirs. Sorry to say, but you don't own it. You didn't make it and you can't take it and replace it for your feelings. It doesn't work like that. And thank goodness it doesn't. Imagine if we owned everyone's feelings about us. You don't have to feel bad if someone doesn't like you, or good if they do. If you think about it, human emotions are unique signatures. No two people love the same way.

Here's an experiment: next time you hug someone, think about your feelings about them. What do they mean to you? How do they make you feel? And then imagine the energy coming toward you. How do they feel about you? What do you mean to them? How do you make them feel? It's intuitive that your and another's feelings would be different. It's coming from different people. So now you can own your own feelings, and face whatever emptiness you feel at the thought of not literally having the love of another. This love that fills this void is the love you generate for others and for yourself.

"Remember that wherever your heart
is, there you will find your treasure." –
Paolo Coelho, The Alchemist

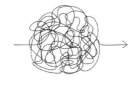

CHAPTER 6

Facing Your Vow

What do we do when we come face-to-face with our marriage vows? Personally, this one haunted me. The tribulation surrounding this voice in the back of my mind was perhaps the hardest thing for me to overcome. However hellacious it was to work though, finding resolution was the key of moving forward. It must be addressed, and you do have to answer the hard question, "Did I do everything I could in service of our marriage?" I honestly can't imagine how I would feel coming up to a chapter like this one in a book. Depending where you are in your journey, you may feel anything from anger to deep sadness to guilt. You may want to skip this chapter altogether or you may be awaiting the part that reveals the solution to this painful question. Whatever you are feeling, hang in there with me, because it is finding the solution to this that enables you to become crystal clear on how you choose to move forward with your partner in question, as well as soothing any anxiety you may have, providing you a sense of confidence and loving peace unlike anything you have experienced in this uncoupling journey to date.

When we get married, the vow is to stay with each other through thick and thin. Anything that comes your way, you and your husband find a way to rise above it, weathering all the storms in life. It provides a couple a tremendous amount of strength because it requires both people to push through personal obstacles and grow. When we do triumph, we enjoy an unbelievable coming together. But what happens when we don't or we can't? We know a lot of married couples that side stepped important issues, don't we? I know couples celebrating fortieth anniversaries of marriages you couldn't pay me to be in. The quality of your relationship matters more than the years you pass together, and it matters more than if you stay together or if you don't. No matter what your marital status in the future, your relationship with your future ex continues as does whatever quality is your standard. It's simply the evolution of your relationship and your fulfillment of your work in this life together. It doesn't end if your marriage does.

A successful marriage is not one where you don't get divorced. I cringe when I hear the statistic that (does everyone say it?) half of marriages end in divorce...like it's code for "divorce is a failed marriage." And as for the half of the marriages that live their lives together until death? How many couples do you know that have made it to old age, truly in love with one another? It happens! It's just a small percentage. And of the marriages that end in divorce? How many of those marriages made the choice to uncouple out of love for one another, and remained dear to one another until death? It's a very small but growing percentage. This, in my mind, is a successful union as much as the couples that had the uncomplicated business of staying together. It is true, that most of us experience love and marriage to be rather difficult with some pretty serious bumps in the road. No matter the experience, it is a fertile ground for growth and learning, a sacred space of the most intimate nature.

When my husband said he was leaving me, I knew it was out of desperation. I knew that it was out of sadness and insecurities. I knew he was spinning. I was both devastated and relieved because I had worked so hard to make things come together in the way we needed them to without success. It had been eating up all our energy and time for years, even stealing a substantial time away from our children. By the end, I felt like I wasn't even the mother I wanted to be because I was so busy saving my marriage that I wasn't helping children with schoolwork, nor cooking, and some mornings locked in private conversations without making breakfast, or watching after them like I knew I needed to. At times it was so very difficult and upsetting. At the time of separation, I was the person that was emotionally stable and because of this I felt a responsibility knowing he wasn't in a good state of mind. However, he was an adult and I couldn't continue to override him by telling him what was best for him or for us. In our relationship, I tended to do the thinking for us as a couple, with the best of intentions but I became aware of how it was insidiously detrimental to our partnership, and so learned to back off and let Ben think and do for himself.

In the first few months after he told me it was over, he was spiraling, meeting women and hoping to find what he had been missing in our relationship only to be horribly disappointed and scared. He would come back to me unsure if he should really leave me. I had to make a boundary because I couldn't take the yo-yo. After all, my focus had turned completely to my children and it was my commitment to provide stability for them during this rocky time. I told him, somewhat reluctantly, exactly the things I would need to happen before I would get back together with him. You see, if you tell your partner your needs, all of them explicitly, they can turn around and meet them. This potentially can put you in the very difficult situation of working things out when you've already emotionally detached. So, it took *a lot* of courage for me to say exactly what he would have to do for me to reengage and work on our marriage together again. To my utter surprise, he didn't do any of them. He didn't even try. I was shocked. But by being vulnerable, I was able to learn something that was a significant game changer. I learned that he wasn't serious about making it work with me, it was for him, a solution to his emptiness. Putting in the effort wasn't part of the plan. This happened another few times, and each time I reluctantly reminded him of exactly what he would have to do. I could not recommit with someone that wasn't serious about recommitting. Every time I had courageously delivered my requirements, it was me living true to my vow.

Another interesting piece of this story is that after he left me, I asked if we may just be separated. I asked if we could keep divorce off the table. We were to be totally separated, moving out into our own homes, having relationships, everything, but for me, I just wasn't sure if divorce was the right way to move forward. I still held out hope that if we had enough space to learn the hard lessons, we could come back together years in the future. He agreed to keeping divorce off the table. And, why not creative alternatives to divorce? Why not give each other a temporary space to do the work that's needed, whether it be separation or something a bit more creative than that? When you are with one person your whole life there's a lot one could explore. Marriage is so many things other than lovers. Most often, it's everything else besides lovers! And in any of those shared realms, one could try a separation to see where you end and the other begins. Some of the difficulty in being with someone since childhood is that you never really experienced yourself on your own. If you have trouble with finances for example, how do you know whose issue it is when all the accounts are shared? Second to intimacy problems were financial issues in my relationship, only stress about money didn't have any bearing in our separation. I had talked for years about separating finances from my husband. I always just equally blamed myself, and yet I couldn't get a handle on it when I watched my end of the monthly spending. Having creativity to safely and honestly experiment in a relationship is necessary if you don't want to just end it. This is the headspace I occupied. I focused on my own growth and wellbeing and holding the ground, taking each day at a time.

However, there did come a day that held the final test of my vow that I will never forget. And for me, this was *the* pivotal moment where I went from asking the universe how to move forward, searching for signs for how to progress in the right direction, to knowing with certainty separation was indeed the way forward. Ben had called me, crying. This time he begged sincerely for me to work on our relationship with him. He sounded more certain and that he would make more of an effort. I reminded him of what I had asked him to do to show me his commitment, which he still had not done. Although he acknowledged what I said, he spoke to me in a way that made me question myself. He begged me to come back. Our call ended saying I would think about it, knowing that he was asking me move forward with him, pushing my requirements aside.

This day I screamed. I screamed bloody murder all day in between sobbing. On my way home, I pulled over on a side street to scream and cry. I strained every muscle and tore through my vocal cords with my heavy deep sobs. I spoke aloud to God looking upward out of total desperation. I didn't know what to do. I knew that if I said yes, I was risking what intuitively felt like another seven years of the three and a half years I had already experienced trying to do the work of two people, of long conversations shutting our children out of the room, of the stress and strain in the bedroom when I had felt I had just come into a newfound sexuality. It was a risk that weighed heavily against my personal development, something very close to my heart after starting a family at a young age and forgoing focus on my personal success. Early the next morning, I was prepared with my answer. I had to know with every cell of my body that I did everything in my power to uphold my vow of marriage until death.

"Yes," I told him.

He looked at me. "What?" he asked.

I replied, "Yes, I thought about it and I've decided I will work on our marriage."

His response blew my mind; it was so unexpected. He said, "I thought you said that we would just be separated for now and see how that goes. Right?"

I kid you not. I asked with innocent and incredulous curiosity, "What did you do last night?"

His answer was just that he hung out on our friend's couch. Whether he did or not meant nothing to me. My question was reflective of my first thought, which was that *something* must have happened that satisfied his need for security. And with that, I knew I had received the answer to move forward. The requirements that I should have never waived in the first place now went out the window. We were separating. I was in charge. The jig was up.

I had fulfilled my vow. I had, in fact, honored our marriage to the very best of my ability. From that moment on, I had a direction and was no longer going to allow myself to be put in that position.

How do you feel about where you stand with your vow? Have you already received your absolute certainty? Do you know the direction that is your next step or is there something that still pulls you back? It's impossible to move forward when you've got an attachment to the past. Give yourself space to identify your hang-ups. Maybe it's not your vow, maybe it's something else, something you gave up, a hurt, or perhaps is a fond memory from happy times. These questions have to be addressed, as scary as they are. The result – should you have the courage to be vulnerable – can surprise you, and knowing that you left no stone unturned gives you unparalleled strength and confidence.

You will not be able to move forward without deciding for yourself what you want to do. If you are on the receiving end of the proposition to divorce as I was, you have a choice and you have to own it. It has to come straight from the heart as an acknowledgment, "Yes, this is the more loving choice for me, too." Then what happens is you are now in a mutual agreement. This is very different than "he left me." "He left me" makes you the victim. Victims feel hurt and anger and blame. The temptation in finding social vindication through being the victim, I'll be the first to admit, is very attractive, but it has severe consequences. It is a choice not to own the part of you that brought you to this point of power, unwittingly choosing to live in a fantasy of your making. Owning one's choice is an honorable struggle. One must manage to be conscious of self-pity and catch wounded utterances when they escape your lips that uphold this victim mentality. If you can change that and throw out reasoning that supports powerlessness and unfairness, it will take a positive shape in legal proceedings, financial situations, and relationships. Given that you will undoubtedly talk with your children many times over with how your divorce came to pass, your choice in the voice you take will have a profound effect on them and their emotional well-being. Will your voice be one of certainty, strength and compassion or will it hint of forfeiture, feebleness and inertia? Think twice before trading present vindication for future prosperity.

Just to bring all of this together in a way you can use and practice, I'm going to suggest some tools to find these answers for yourself, or if you just feel like you want confirmation of what you know, try some of these exercises. If you pay close attention to your feelings as you ask yourself, you will have some immediate under-standing of where you stand and what you need to do to find resolution.

What makes you want to hold on to this relation-ship?

What makes you want to let go of your relationship?

Do you feel angry or upset with your spouse for leaving you?

Do you know that you have a choice beyond what your spouse has done or asked you for?

What is the most loving solution for you?

What are your hang-ups that keep you tied into the past? How can you better face them?

If you left your spouse, do you question your decision? Why? What stone has yet to be turned over? What haven't you faced and explored the possibilities of?

Allow yourself time for your knowing to become clear on *your* decision. When that definitive moment makes itself known, you will be ready to take the driver's seat.

CHAPTER 7

Taking the Driver's Seat

Have you come to a clear understanding about how you choose to move forward in your relationship? And yes, I say move forward, because no matter what the choice you make, it will be the evolution of your relationship, not the end of it. If you still feel unsure or if there is a hint of doubt lurking, it is up to you discover what you need to do to challenge it. Spend some more time in chapter six, tuning into yourself with guided meditations and dream interpretation. Go find a bodyworker or energy worker that works with emotions. Talk with friends or simply talk to yourself over a voice recorder, or is it something that will only find resolution in speaking directly to the source. In the end, it is essential that you find the courage to do what you are afraid of, but what you know you need to do, with honesty and integrity, that will give you the clarity that stares you in the face. This is when heart and head aligns, when peace comes over you, and the moment you will be able to take a step forward with confidence. If you are not there yet, it is with love and patience I tell you not to despair. Stay in the present moment and arrive you will. However, if you have reached this chapter with clarity, it is with celebration that I invite you to take the next step. And it starts with taking control of your life by making your own decisions.

Now that you are crystal clear on how you want to move forward, it's time to fully own that decision. Owning your decision deserves its own step in the process because it's just that crucial. Even though it can be done in one step. In one thought. Are you ready?

Write this in your notebook: It is my decision to.... And fill in the blank. Decorate it. Give it it's own page. You will want to revisit that page in your journal every time you want to pull the victim card going forward with anger, fear and resentment. All your words and actions will support the ownership of your choice if you wish to step into your full power to take life in your own direction.

Setting the Course of Action and Making Boundaries

You may have a spouse who's mentally and emotionally spinning, who hasn't yet found clarity of direction and if that's the case, you want to take over the wheel if they've been directing things so far. Emotions like anger, frustration and aggression pointed your way also speak of a loss of control and insecurity, even though they are disguised as control. A calm and collected energy, patient and kind is always the one in charge and makes anything else look like immaturity. Never be intimidated by immaturity, it only affirms you have the upper hand. You are in control of yourself and are free to make your own decisions and personal boundaries.

One can do this with a simple conversation. And it goes just this way:

"Because of (this) I have decided (this) and from now on (this is what will be focused on) or (this will or will not be an option)."

Here's mine so you get the idea:

"After I screamed all day to decide whether or not I could throw myself back into making our marriage work without you meeting my needs, I realized that it is best for me that we separate like we talked about. And from now on, it is not an option to try to make it work. Don't come back to me asking me this again. It is a no. You've been driving this thing for a while, and now I want you to know that you no longer have a choice in the matter. I'm driving now. Think of it this way: it takes the burden off of you to make up your mind. It's much easier to be handed change than to choose it. I'm going to make things really simple. We are selling this house, moving into separate houses, dating who we want, and totally separated moving forward."

That is nearly word for word the conversation I had. The power he felt like he had in the situation made him bonkers because he was not in the right mind to make decisions. His fears were driving him in circles. It was hard for him to hear that it was final and that he no longer had a choice in the matter, but ultimately it gave him some peace. You have to be exceptionally clear, calm, and in control, and it has to truly come from the ground up within you. You won't be able to fake it. Your energy through your gaze will convey it without a doubt. You must make clear boundaries. You lay out the plan and the expectations. It is with firmness and care. Anger is an emotion that immediately conveys lack of control. Anger is powerlessness, and if you are wrestling with this, I invite you to go do some gorgeous, very human work so that you can come back to center, back into your power and the ability to clearly communicate the plan. Have as many conversations as you need to and find your voice if you go.

I had a dream that illustrated this. Dreams are great because they let you know right where you are at the moment, and even what to expect. In my dream, I got out of the passenger side of a car, walked around the car, and told my husband I was driving. The road ahead was like a rollercoaster road. It was a steep decline at first, and in the distance went up and back down. It was a little treacherous but I knew I was capable and took the wheel. My husband got out of the car, and as I got in, it was my mother sitting in the passenger's side, who had become a best friend of mine by this time in my life. In my dream, I handed her a glass of wine and told her to buckle up. It's pretty easy to understand and it's kind of funny. I had other driving dreams as well. Steep inclines, bumps, obstacles, and near accidents. Obviously, the road symbolizes the path in front of you. You can trust your dreams to help you navigate what lies just ahead.

It's good to note that being in the driver's seat does not imply you are making decisions for your spouse. Nowhere in this book will you find advice to be controlling. The car your husband was previously driving was yours that you let him drive. Your road ahead is yours. You're just no longer allowing anyone to take you in a direction you don't want to go. There are so many times in life where we go along with things without bothering to ask ourselves if that's our desire, too. When you have dreams where someone else is driving, it's not a bad thing, it just means that they're taking the lead and you're following along, maybe because you didn't have a better idea or you don't know what else to do. That's pretty normal in a relationship. There's a natural exchange, allowing one another to make decisions for each other and sometimes making creative compromises. It's preferable to not always have one person that dictates what restaurant you eat at or what kind of movies you watch when you're together, or what kind of music is listened to in the house. If you are changing the music when someone gets in the car with you, or if you give up eating what you like because your spouse doesn't like it, I'd argue that there is room for self-love and self-expression yet. The solution to that is simple. Don't change the radio station, put olives in the pasta, and opt for your independent foreign language film without asking. At this stage in the game, I am probably giving you advice about your future relationship or best friend. My point being, you have the power to live the life you want, but you have to be willing to put yourself out there and make choices that get you on the road to where you want to be.

Now that you have taken the driver's seat which starts with a shift in self-perception and have the conversation that lets you lovingly inform your partner of how you will be moving forward, you'll find yourself stepping out of this most unsettling initial phase. Even though there is much to contend with moving forward, having a direction of your own choice without the nagging inner self-doubts will simplify your experience and give you an advantage.

For further clarity, you are invited to ponder these questions:

What are your needs going forward?

What are some goals you would like to focus on?

How do you see life in the next few months?

What kind of schedule do you want to keep?

What daily rituals do you have to keep you focused and grounded?

What do you need to do before you get started on your plan?

What leeway and safe space will you provide yourself should you find yourself feeling vulnerable and how would you like to comfort and nurture yourself?

By taking your life's direction in your hands, you begin a new adventure. Once you start to get organized with all the practical to-do's in the near future, you will be aware that this is fertile ground for creating a future you desire. You are in a place where you are asking yourself broad questions regarding where you want to live, for example. You may be curious if a new person will enter your life. You will feel the power in the choices you have to make. So, the first stop I want to take you from here is into a place where your true spirit resides without limitation, because even though life is full of present limitations, we do much better making our immediate decisions if we know what we want long-term, even if we cannot foresee how they would ever work out beyond winning the lottery. Where you stand now, hands on the steering wheel and eyes on the road, know there will be opportunities that come up you have never been presented with before. We will now prepare you so that not only will you be able to steer yourself in a direction toward deep fulfillment, but your senses will be primed to act on your dreams when the conditions are just right.

CHAPTER 8

Remembering Pocketed Dreams

In this chapter lies the major underlying reason for the unexpected change in your life's path. When you came into existence, there was special meaning to your life. You are totally unique. Your interests, your style, your skills, your voice ... all your attributes collide within you, combine, and radiate outward as expression, interaction and service to the world. You have certainly been on the path of fulfilling your life's purpose and that is exactly the reason why you find yourself here – with the power to shape your future in unprecedented ways. Never before has there been a time when it has been so vital that you know your deepest desires. As you work through the daily tasks of deconstructing your life, you become completely available to the actualizations of the law of attraction. If this expression "law of attraction" is new to you, I recommend you immerse yourself in the teachings every day. There will be space for you that didn't exist for you before, and with this, the chance to live out your dreams. What do you dream of? There may be some that you can tell me off the top of your head, yet others might be buried way deep down. Mostly because when you dreamt them, they were considered unreasonable or so unlikely to happen you might consider them to be impossible and so forgotten. After seasons come and go, after the rain and snow and landslides and whatnot, your dream is no longer on the tip of your tongue, or, as I put it, nicely folded and put into your breast pocket, ready to be plucked if the opportunity arise. This is the chapter where we unearth those forgotten dreams. We will bring them to the surface and breathe new life into them. We can't throw to the side and forget what it is we deeply desire. It is our hearts song.

First let's get the surface ones written and out in the open by journaling. All you can think of. Especially the crazy ones, the dumb ones, and the impossible ones. Those are essential to write down. You can mark the subject line with this:

"Dreams I kept in mind."

Here are some examples of my pocketed dreams: Move to someplace beautiful and cultural. Learn nine languages, get into amazing physical shape, live in a hobbit house, play the piano, write a symphony, write a book exploring the meaning of spirals, learn ballet, do a scorpion pose, travel the world, learn to sail, be a millionaire.

Okay, now that we've written down all the ones that we can think of, create another space for the ones that come to you later. They might come as you read this chapter, or in your dream tonight. They might come to you in the middle of work when you can't write it down right away so you're going to have to be prepared with some kind of memorizing method lest you miss your chance to add it to this list. They pop into your consciousness, as if they are remembering you, rather than you remembering them. Your next subject line reads:

"Unearthed dreams."

Now, let's think back to your transformation, the one you had before the proverbial poop hit the fan with your marriage. There were probably quite a few ratcheting elements at work for you. Let's make a note about all we learned about ourselves through those elements and the catalyst, with a subject line that reads:

"Who I found out I am."

Here's who I found out I am: I am beautiful and vibrant. I am sensual and passionate. I love lingerie – when they fit me. I have a strong athletic body. I want to be with someone who is optimistic and positive, and as strong as I am.

After I separated with my husband, I remembered that I had always wanted to move someplace where I felt more connected to the land and the culture. I knew that once we split up and we meet new people and make new relationships, the chance of moving someplace I loved would plummet. While together, he would never consider moving. So, in a moment of inspiration and as a last-ditch attempt to realize my dream, I asked we to move away to the same town, what with having kids together and all. Nantucket, I suggested. No, was the answer. No matter. I moved onto to the afternoon. I had to get ready for work. As I drove through the familiar and pretty deciduous canape on my way in, I remembered my number one place, buried and forgotten, as I failed to mention it earlier in the day. My dream unearthed was to live in France.

I texted Anais, my au pair turned great friend. I told her I missed her and I wished to visit her in France. I didn't know if it were possible. It had never been a possibility in the past, but I was about to finally receive insurance money from my personal loss from the accident. I got a text back. She wrote me, "I would love that! You have to let me know if you can come, and then maybe I can take the summer off and we can travel all over the country and stay with friends and family." I couldn't believe it! I had long dreamt of summers in France. In fact, one of my clients once said to me years before, and quite seriously, that I should spend a summer there. Like I could afford it ... did she even know how her warm suggestion crushed me? It was obvious to me that we had different means, and she wasn't in touch with a middle class lifestyle, I thought. And here I was, offered quite seriously to spend a summer in France with my dear friend, the impossible possible. Yes! I wanted that!

I asked Ben, "What if I spent the summer with the kids in France? I can give you space to figure out your stuff. The house could stay clean while it was on the market, and you could get out of your parent's house and move in ... hopefully it will sell before we get back and the kids could be distracted with other things than us separating."

He said yes! It suited his needs. I'll add this special note for good measure – the night that I booked this epic adventure, before I tapped the final button confirming purchase of our flights, I called Ben and I told him, very reluctantly, "I am about to book this trip. Are you sure that it is okay with you." Why? I had already gotten his permission a few weeks earlier, and talked about it a few times since ... but I asked because I knew it was right to make sure beforehand, so that there weren't any issues and I was completely confident. And, again, he said yes. I clicked and took a big deep breath. Wouldn't you know that three months later, a week before the trip

I got a phone call from Ben. He started, "About the trip ..." Oh God, I thought.

"I don't think I'm okay with you going," he continued.

The risky triple check I did before buying our plane tickets paid off big time. I said with authentic confidence and poise, "I'm sorry, Ben. I asked you if you were extra sure right before I booked, and I did that to cover all my bases. You told me to go ahead and I did."

He remembered and knew I was in the right. I did my best to get the *real* answers upfront. I didn't try to slide by undetected like I had considered doing. It takes courage, but it gives you the ability to move forward with confidence.

Anyway, the trip was such a phenomenal experience. Eight weeks of crisscrossing France with a week in the middle to visit friends in Berlin. It has changed me and my children forever in the best way possible. A deep wish of mine came true causing an emergence of confidence that my dreams were in fact obtainable and I was just getting started. All of that would never have been if I hadn't unearthed a deep desire and taken hold of a pocketed dream. Your pocketed dreams are keys. Keep them within an arms-length and be ready to try to open a few locks. Expect a few to stay shut too before you find a fit. Just giving it a go gets the energy rolling in the right direction. You have to talk about your dreams all the time. Contrary to what you think, it's not money that you need. People are your biggest resources. It's momentum that comes from your energy, your conversations, and it's the people you meet that help make your dreams come true. There are moments of opportunity that arise out of thin air, sometimes coming directly from a momentary thought you have followed by a single question texted to a friend. Just remember this, the first and most crucial step is knowing exactly what you want in life.

It's really important you don't poopoo your ideas and dreams. That would make them not happen. And It's also really important that in your mind when you think of them, you don't place a fence between you and your dream. And what I mean by that is, don't think about what you want but in the same breath, separate yourself from it in some way. Here's how you know if you are doing that: When you think of what you desire, you actually feel bad, not good. No wonder you feel sad. You are denying yourself what you want most. Just imagine removing the mental boundary. Now it's just you holding the thing you desire, united somewhere in time and space, and this little key gets put in your pocket. We don't try to manhandle things to make them happen either. When the window presents itself, it's as easy as jumping though. You might need a stool or someone to push you up so that you can reach it, but it's pretty simple. Anxiety, impatience, sadness, and fear just get in the way of you seeing your window. You have to keep your head clear and every day be in the present moment and in communication with your inner voice. You don't want to miss it. If you have the feeling like you did miss it, you really won't have to worry, there will be many more to come. Like a train, just wait for the next one to come and when it does, don't hesitate. If you really want to live your dream, you have to take them seriously.

For now, just look to get into the flow. Get into a nice daily rhythm. Show up in life aware and attentive. Pay attention to the signs and symbols all around you and harmonize with your surroundings. That's when the world opens up to you.

And how do you want to live your life? To start, it is a continuation of the life you lived that includes all the things you loved and that you'd like to take forward with you. You don't have to give up any of your familiar favorite things just because they seem to belong to you as a couple. I suggest watching the family home movies, listening to the special songs, and visiting favorite places sans guilt. Those places belong to you. They aren't places and things that have to remain in the past. If you have an album that you personally love, that happens to take you back to a time in high school, automatically that stuff seems off limits as does favorite vacation spots that only belonged to you as a couple. There are bound to be hundreds of these kinds of special "off-limits" our-thing things. Contrary to what you think, they weren't all meant to stay in the beginning timeframe of your life. Bring any of those things into your new life that you like. They are your places, things, and songs. Their meanings extend into the future. They change with you. It's good to bring them forward. Keep seeing those bands in concert and allow them to expand their meaning. They were in fact meant to take part in your life to a greater extent if you like them to. And beyond that? Explore every day the statement of how you wish to live your life and allow yourself to expound on it.

For me, I know how I want to live my life. I want to live it with freedom and adventure. I want to love on my children every day. And I want to sumptuously eat up all the pleasures in life that always make every day beautiful, especially when it's tough. Whether you can verbalize how you want to live your life or not, you are encoded with the answers. On that level you know exactly what the life you desire feels like, and it's up to your mind to figure out how to live it. It's in the little decisions you make every day and it's in the big fat ones you make when a window of opportunity opens a world to you.

We get so hung up in what we don't know, we don't stop to ask ourselves what we do know. And we get so stuck thinking about what we don't want that we fail to ask ourselves what we do want. If you ever find yourself stuck in this trap where you are focused on what you don't know and feeling upset about it, the exercise I suggest doing is asking yourself what *do* you know, what *can* you do, and how *do* you get what you want and journal on that. This is the key to breaking through. You know far more than you think.

And this brings us to the final pitfall, fear. You can't see through fear. Fear is like driving your car with a coating of mud over the windshield. It's all you can see. And you don't know if it's mud on your windshield or if it's just really dark outside. It's mud. And you'll never see what is really in front of you, unless you take the mud off. It's just impossible. So stop trying, you can't see! Take a look at what you *do* see, which are your fears. See them for what they are, work them through until you are no longer afraid, and what lies beyond will become crystal clear.

With or without your marriage, you need to make choices that feel good for you. Having survived divorce by compassionately uncoupling, I can share with you the rainbow that comes after the downpour. I have reached this place of friendship with my ex-husband, seeing glimmers of future possibilities of how our relationship may take shape in really cool, unexpected ways. I am able to see and understand things I hadn't when we were married. I am currently engaged to be married with someone that lights me up. Our combined children love each other and the family we created. It's a pleasure for me to see them happily thriving with school, friends and personal interests. I have been thriving. I've been to Europe countless times now, speaking French and feeding my spirit. Having been officially divorced two years, in entering the third year of my post-divorce period, I'm thigh deep in an extremely exciting part of my life. I'm opening my professional life up in ways I've only dreamt of. Things are quickly taking off and there is so much to enjoy and so much to look forward to. I want to be there for your story. I want to know where you would like to go from here. You can get there and I can show you how. Follow me through these next chapters as we shine a light into the dark corners of your life as it exists now and illuminate the live you want to live.

CHAPTER 9

Your Life Starts to Take Shape

What can we expect when it comes to our new life? How do we even approach it? No matter what your story is, divorce is traumatic. We gracefully are shattered in a million little fragments, and for a while, unsure about how to pick up the pieces. So, it's with sensitivity and an underlying anticipation that we explore what to expect in your new life, with the intention of giving you a level of comfort in knowing what is to come is largely up to you.

Nearly every aspect of your life potentially changes around the time of divorce. It is a time of letting go and a time of invitation for new to come in. In the heart of this small cyclone is your relationship. For your entire life, it has been with your childhood sweetheart. And now, this space is open. There is no need to fill it. You are whole in and of yourself, but it stands out as the most significant free space in your life, with the possibilities that meet you right where you are. It would seem as soon as the empty spaces appear, the opportunities to fill them in present themselves. It is evident that everyone has their own timeline, starting with some of us whose relationships start so soon they overlap the last, leaving no alone time in between. For others, their desire to focus on their children or fulfill another area of their life, overshadows the desire to partner with someone, which arrives later on when it becomes available to the world.

Uncoupling a longtime partnership is a unique and interesting position to be in. To understand deeply what that space is, we'll consider the foundational idea that this life was not the first with your childhood sweetheart, and within the pages of your soul's story, you may have met a natural ending for the time being. If this idea indeed resonates with you, it will be a puzzle piece that snaps into place, adding an extra layer of peace, and the ability to shift your gaze forward. Most definitely this is a space of opportunity to liberate our self-expression like never before. And should you be ready presently for a new love in your life, how do you find them? How do we avoid the pitfalls? There is a lovely conversation we have with ourselves where we get very specific about what we will accept in our new lives based on our personal desires. I will share with you secrets in how to open up to receiving what you want when you're ready for it and how to read the signs around you that point in the direction of yes.

Soul Contracts

When we find someone so young, we can consider the idea that it isn't our first go around with them. Is it easy for you to imagine many past lives with your ex? In the middle of facing my divorce, a woman told her story in those words. She told me she had been given the insight into her divorce being that she had lived many lifetimes with her husband learning and growing in specific ways, and now it was time to uncouple. It made me reflect on my own. What was the energy behind my partnership? What past lifetimes might we have shared? Was this a natural ending?

A story of my son comes to mind when I think about the possibility that we might come into this life awaiting to continue a relationship from another time and place. When Archer was six, he woke up and ran to me quite upset and told me of a dream that was so real to him, he couldn't differentiate his experience from real life. He told me he met a girl he loved so much and that he needed to ask her to marry him. He begged me to leave the house right away to take him to buy some flowers. He needed them to propose to her. He told me he just had to find her. "How will I find her?" he asked. He exploded with the idea to drive around the neighborhood until we spotted her. The moment he realized the gap between his waking life and the one he just left, he was utterly defeated. I watched his posture slump and throw himself down in loss. She was out of reach. I don't begin to explain what exactly had occurred, but it felt mysterious and real.

I was introduced to the idea of soul contracts by Caroline Myss around the time of my great awakening, years before separation and divorce. I enjoyed her perspective. She shares her understanding in her language about the bigger picture in life. We need some kind of big picture framework to ground this wild experience in a way that makes complete sense of it all. The result is this deeply stable base of peace. If we open ourselves up to beyond the physical world, it reveals itself to us, it comforts us and becomes an active part of our reality.

There may be ways you think of tapping into this knowledge already, and if you're not sure how but this interests you to learn more, an avenue will certainly appear to you and draw you into this knowledge. Personally, I make a habit to act on little thoughts that pop in my head, should I feel compelled. I might run into a new store, or end up finding information on a spiritual energy reader and get a yes inside me to experience more about something I come across. You may connect with an intuitive person, or listen to a book that talks about the world that envelops our own. Take what you want from the experience. The information is for you to do with what you want. No one has the answers but you. But some people are really good at tuning into other energies and they are even better when they can express what they feel in a way that's true to source. We are all filters of this energy, and our energy infuses in the message, no matter how gifted the intuitive, know that the message will taste like the bottle from which you drank it.

Being Alone and Wholeness

There is a cornucopia of emotions that come up around being alone. How does this very subject matter sit with you? Myself, I have not experienced a lot of un-coupled time in my life, though it is clear to me that being coupled or not doesn't have a lot of bearing on the emotion of loneliness. One easily can feel lonely in a relationship, and quite comfortable without a partner, being our first clue that the key to finding relief of this plaguing emotion is turning our focus to within ourselves, available to us today. Though I tend to be emotionally independent in my relationships – sometimes to a fault – I did spend between the ages of ten and thirty-something in and out of a deep state of gut-aching longing, until the day it was revealed to me how to let go of it.

Longing is the mother of loneliness. It can turn its focus on any particular desire you have. It is a feeling of loss, of sadness, and of emptiness. For me, I longed for a place that felt like home. I felt it every time I came back from out of town. I was searching, until I had a dream where I was doing just that, walking through cities and down lengthy stretches of sidewalk, through prairieland and up a look tower to find what at that view-point, looked like a needle in a haystack. Afterward, I shared my dream with an intuitive woman who told me this astonishing revelation. I *was* the searching. I had to sit with that for a moment before I could wrap my brain about what that meant for me. If I wanted to stop searching for the thing I longed for, I simply had to stop looking. I had to trust that all is available to me and that I am whole and that everything happens according to a law of perfection. What is, is. Why is it that all of the most profound lessons in life are so damned simple? They're simple to the point that they're easily missed and really hard to explain. And, my favorite part is how when you *really* get it, this simple lesson of: I am the searching, so stop searching and you will become something other than that, when you tell others, their response is something like, yeah no duh. It makes me laugh. No really, what is, is. And what is not, is not. How high do I sound? But this is what truth sounds like. Hard to put in writing, but I'm banking on you being open to it.

And now that we're done searching, because we decided it so, what do we do with this hole in my heart that prompted the search in the first place? My seeing woman told me, leave it empty and fill it with God. So, I breathed deeply into this pit, filling it with divine will and energy. I have never experienced longing since. I want things, but I believe they exist for me. I simply align myself with higher will, do my best work. I believe always that good things are here, and will continue to come. I hold my dreams in my breast pocket to guide my way.

Liberate Yourself

There is a magnificent opportunity in life when a great cycle comes to a close, and whole new cycle begins. It is the chance to be more yourself than you've ever been. Before, everything had been structured with a prevailing mentality and a way to think, speak, and behave. You had your place in life that on some level you agreed upon. Now is a chance to truly reinvent yourself, presenting yourself to new social circles, to new family ... and to your own image in the mirror. You are able to present yourself as the person you wish to be, or better said, as the person you truly are.

You likely won't need a lot of guidance in this department. Schedule into your calendar the things you love to do, seeing and working with people who you'd like to pass time, and change your body, health, and style in a way that suits you. Don't put pressure on yourself. Your goal is to enjoy the process. It's making the progress that lights us up and fills us with enthusiasm, and *that* can start day one.

And now that you've been considering ways you'd like to outwardly express yourself, I'll ask you, how do you want to live day to day? What things do you spend your time doing, if you can do anything? I recently asked myself the question, what makes a happy life? Is it the vacations? The memories? It seems to me the answer is that it's the quality of enjoyment in our *daily* lives, since life in full includes every moment you are alive. At work, at home, eating, making love, taking kids to school, reading, doing the dishes... for a truly happy life all these times would be more or less happy.

So, I asked my children about specific people in their lives, if they thought those people had happy lives:

Does grandma have a happy life? When you imagine grandma does she look happy? Does dad have a happy life? When you see him in your head for that split second, what is he doing? Is he smiling? And on I went. They enjoyed the exercise. Fascinating. These little first mental snapshots of the of the people in question will give you a definite sense of how your children experience these people and their happiness or lack thereof in acceptably unexciting, and un-notable daily life.

Then you may have the courage to ask, how do you see me? What am I doing? Do I have a happy life?

It sort of reminds me of the comical moments where kids are playing dolls and you hear the mom doll yelling at her kids all the time, and you think to yourself wow, is that what I sound like? Um, yes. But don't fret. You get to consciously choose how you want to show up in the lives of your children and of others and it is never too late to show up in more ways we want.

Changing Your Daily

Where you walk, you go.

I heard that, and as simple as it is, it made *so much sense*. I thought to myself, "I want to walk through London and Paris." It's not that I wanted to vacation to these places; I wanted Europe to be part of my life. So, in holding this outlandish dream in close to my heart and my mind, unbelievable opportunities have arisen for me- opportunities I had a hand in creating. Since the summer I spent in France I have been out of the country every six months. Travel to Europe has been part of my new life and most recently, my eyes opened to how I will make it even more integrated into a common experience, by becoming my work. At the time that my future shown through to white canvas, this was completely out of reach. Hold space for new activities in your routine.

What life does your true self live?

Allow yourself to daydream on this and more. Choose the questions that stick out to you to ponder in your journal.

What would a happy life for you look like?

What brings you the most joy, smiles and laughter?

What do you imagine doing if you thought of yourself in full play like a kid?

Come up with a few scenarios for that one- how else do you imagine goofing off, heart light and silly?

What simple things do you appreciate around you?

What little gift could you give yourself today?

What person could you sit and think about all the things you adore about them? And if you desire to, send them a love note.

Life is what you make of it. Enjoy the challenges you put before you and take frequent breaks to center yourself, breathe and integrate. Balance challenging yourself with relaxing, patting your head a good job and kissing your own hand, no matter what the outcome.

How to Meet Someone Special

It takes a whole lot of courage to invite someone new into your life which could very well include new children should this someone come as a package of people to love. This is within our scope of choice, which is amazing when you think about it. You may not choose who it is that you bump into, but you most definitely have a choice in who you stick with. And every experience allows you to check in with your inner compass, and where you stand in relation to your personal north.

The meaning you give your experiences shape them and they, in turn, shape you. This dance will require you to know precisely what you want while you stay open to the energy of the person you bumped into a date with. If it turns out there is a draw for you in this other person, be ready to face your personal fears that undoubtedly will present themselves quite forwardly after just coming through a monumental separation. This is normal and healthy and you will find yourself through it, take comfort. And with my most loving, motherly tone I will tell you that you might as well get your fears out of the way, because they are inevitable. Just honor your feelings. Each step on the way is at your own pace.

Facing Fears That Hold You Back

Two most common worries that stand to get in your way while taking your brave first foot forward is a worry to choose the wrong direction, the wrong person, the wrong job, etc. The second fear is to repeat a "mistake" from the past that will cause you to relive past pain. Let us go ahead and clear those two fears right off the bat that will stall you, block you and bring you misery. Both those ideas are built on a false premise that there is a possibility of this actually happening, when I would argue their literal impossibilities, and how to see this common misconception on your own terms that allows you freedom to follow through with the right direction and without recreating a prior painful dynamic.

There exists not a direction that doesn't serve its purpose, in at the very least redirecting you in even some small, exacting way. We have this idea that we can regress, or step laterally but it is an idea that is not mandatory to entertain and ultimately invites doubt and despair in your life. Consider the philosophy that there is technically no other direction but forward. There is past and present, and your future comes to meet you where you are, like standing in a stream that continuously comes forward to you. It's a one-way game. When people speak of sideways and backward what they are referring to is their expectations for their present life not matching with their reality. If you find yourself in this place, it may be recognized as a moment when the compass came out of the pocket and the need for simply facing a new direction acknowledged. Any direction you face will walk you forward on your path. Trust in the beauty that we naturally gravitate to the situations that will allow us maximum benefit, because they meet us right where we are.

Consider of the belief of making the same mistake twice quite literally for a moment. In order to make the same mistake you'd need to go back in space and time with the same mentality and people with their mentalities and relive the past. Obviously not going to happen. This means that all your experiences *will* be different, and will ultimately hold different meaning for you. When we see outward patterns, it can be a great tool for looking within, but if you are the kind of person that tends to get into your head and spin around for a while, I would caution you not to get caught into the similarities of your present situation to your past. When you're a hammer, everything looks like a nail, they say. This focus can pull you pretty off center rather quickly. Getting into your head and looking for similarities is likely *itself* a pattern with the purpose to keep you safely immobilized. Ironic, isn't it? My best advice is to put it in your notebook for introspection, and then forget about it and let the answers that you need to break old patterns come to you. You can be assured they will make themselves known.

Once you embrace the reality that takes out the pressures and graveness we live by and attach our-selves to, you will see the reality is much more forgiving and light, and in this world you are strong and resilient. You step confidently forward in any direction, well I say any direction but the truth is there is just one direction that you will go, and that's the direction that you feel most inclined to go. So, it's not as random as you think. In fact, it's not random at all. At a given time, place, phys-ical-mental-emotional constitution and context with all of its variables fixed in that instant, there is only one way it will go. That is the direction it does, in fact, go in. And with that overly simple truth, I will lead into my philosophy behind perfection and how this will give you the confidence to make the hard decisions with ease.

Trusting in Perfection

When you are uncoupling, you make many very important decisions. It is easy to feel the pressure to make the right decision, as we know that what and who we invite into our lives has a profound effect on what we experience, and quite honestly there's a little bit of post traumatic stress hanging around yet to put to rest. Self-doubt can easily sneak in and play havoc in your new playground. I want to give you my philosophy that eliminates self-doubt and allows decision making to be easy and sure. You can trust in the perfection of the way things happen, all the time, if you move past the idea that there are elements of chance, random, and coincidence in your life, into the realm of self-organizing, purposeful, and synchronistic.

What is odd about this list of words is that they are all basically synonyms. It's largely a question of semantics or how you interpret the meaning of these words. All the words speak of unpredictability and simultaneous occurrences, but for me, the difference is whether the phenomenon is based on a lack of organization of the universe or based on the natural laws organizing the universe. As I had previously mentioned, if you could take into consideration the billions of elements interacting between yourself and another person you're considering dating for example, in one given moment, the outcome would look a lot less random and much more synchronized, like a chemical reaction of school chemistry experiment through a microscope, as you saw in slow motion long lines of reflexes falling like dominos at the speed of light between you both, all based on the elements at work, most of which we are not conscious of. The result is true to what exists. In the case of your date, it's phenomenal or it sucks, or you feel confused and bewildered- whatever you feel and consequently decide, it's perfect. Trust it. As your thought patterns evolve, your new beliefs interacts with the world differently, creating very different outcomes. From the perspective of a total self-organizing universe based on strings of natural reactions that are true to each domino in line, you can trust with absolute certainty that everything happens for a reason, as the saying goes. And it's influenced by your very constitution. How does this help you make decisions? Because you can trust that you will ultimately make the decision that is in line with your internal dominos. You lean in the direction of what is right for you, naturally, and can trust that every decision you make is right for the situation, for that moment in time, to fulfill the most significant purpose there is to be had. You will make the choice you are going to make, even if it's not to make a choice at all.

Which leads me to the next observation of the miniscule with huge implications, I don't believe in almost. It's a favorite dispute. People look at me with their heads cocked to the side like a confused pup. *I don't believe in almost.* It either happened or it didn't happen.

In order for it to be almost, it's like it had to happen and not happen at the same time, which I think speaks more to the experience of imagining something happening, but, to your surprise, it didn't. You thought it was. The reality is, there was never a chance it were going to happen, because it didn't. Again, what does this abstract understanding mean for uncoupling? Consider the idea of fantasizing on other outcomes other than what happened being a drain of your time and energy, merely an indulgence to feel a fear that may serve you in an illusionary way to protect you. To reminisce about the past happening other than how it in fact manifested is an excellent way to keep yourself paralyzed in your decision making.

Last element of perfection I'd like to introduce is based on the law of atomic bonding. I look at people and their bonding in the same light, only we're a mass of countless atoms behaving more or less as one, with all the qualities that allow us to bump into one another, stick or repel, with different levels of intensity. Change the external conditions and the relationships between atoms can change. One can trust in the law that enables atoms to behave the way they do. I trust deeply in the fact, that our interactions and our sticking ability are related to this perfection. In a relationship, if there's not enough binding you together, it isn't. If there is, whether you like it or not, it is. There are a lot of reasons we bind together with others, benefiting us in many ways. You could categorize it into healthy or unhealthy reasons if you wanted, but I would argue that it doesn't much matter. What I value is growth, and no matter what is between you and another, you're sure to get that in the perfect way for you. Ah, and how this brings a sense of gratitude!

Because of these simple rules, you can trust that things happen the way they do for a reason and that you can just roll in the direction of ease with confidence. Trust your heart completely, and turn off the minds manufacturing of unfounded hallucinations. If this is a well-worn pattern for you, it is an excellent time to hold space for new patterns to come forth that serve you better.

Finding Courage

Courage is to break through the mainstream belief systems by following your own truth. The way to find true courage I have found is to defeat shame. A recent breakthrough of mine was the connection between embarrassment and shame. When I grew up I understood guilt. My mom talked a lot about that one. I could identify it and was able to pick it out, but shame ... that was like the scarlet letter, right? That was when society looked down their noses at you for getting pregnant out of wedlock, getting a divorce, or being gay. Gratefully, all of which the general public is becoming more accepting of. Shame, I thought, is something my parents' generation and generations before experienced. I probably had felt it, but I don't know when. Until I came to a place in my life where I had to find courage to take action I wanted.

I was working on my business. It was time to settle down into a home, which for me came a bit later in my process. And I was just about to settle on a house that was too small to meet my family's need with the mind frame that everyone can just deal. Until the day I spoke to the sky and declared, I'll take a house in this neighborhood! I was passing through a pretty neighborhood with homes out of my price range. And that's when I stopped and asked myself. What would it take to be able to afford to live here? How much money a year would I need to make? My income up until this point strongly reflected part-time work, stay-at-home mom. And that's when I followed what turned into a string of impulses all starting by finding out the answer to these questions, and making decisions based on what we have discussed in this chapter, the ability to leap because my heart says, "Jump!"

As I became more invested in building my business, and to make more money to support the kind of family life I wanted, it required I became more visible to the public. One day while talking to my life coach, she asked me what was holding me back from this particular task at hand. I said, "I guess I'm afraid to be embarrassed."

And she replied, "Well, you know that embarrassment is shame." And that was the first time I heard that embarrassment, my dear friends, is shame. And it hit me like a ton of bricks. What? Embarrassment is shame? Because I've felt embarrassed aplenty my entire life! In prior generations there was no problem saying detrimental things to keep children in line. Instead of the old fashioned outward shameless shaming, nowadays, we have to manage shaming in these more sneaky, underhanded forms, like sarcasm and teasing. It's an underhanded delivery that is mostly overlooked. Even more difficult to point out as they can hide under the cloak of being a joke. In an environment of shame, we tend to hide our true feelings. For children, they tend not to share anything close to their heart they expect to be teased about. Just as I did when I fell in love at fifteen. Adults tend not to share true feelings when they feel judged for it. Once I recognized this liaison, I've been able to clean up my home of it with a no-shame campaign, as well as within myself when I start to hold myself back for that deep inner fear of humiliation. If you find yourself in a position where you are striving to make unprecedented gains in your new life you are creating, the little trick of banishing shame is exceptionally useful.

To take it one step further, to be worried about an endeavor resulting in embarrassment shows a priority that may be worth changing. For me, it's not as much the result as it is the experience. We all know that all we can do is our very best. The actual results can be mixed. Ultimately, we learn from every endeavor, which makes everything we do worthwhile. But what happens if we disengage from the need to have a certain immediate result and instead focus on the priority of simply experiencing this thing we want to do? We can double our gains, enjoyment plus getting closer to our ultimate goal through learning.

There was a moment when I spoke directly and aloud to this inner voice that lovingly, unobtrusively and covertly held me back with the fear of embarrassment. It did so by politely correcting me, gently pointing out all of the flaws, and whispering non-stop suggestions to improve my work. I became very angry to find myself stuck, not in flow, my efforts progressing in fits and starts with this internal interference, and I had had enough. I had looked at my own reflection in the mirror and demanded to be seen as a person deserving respect and uninterrupted space to be in creative flow. In a nutshell, I went into a tirade, my eyes burning holes into my own gobsmacked expression, my reflection morphing into me outside of me, for five minutes. I yelled, she listened... and after it was over, she apologized and lovingly poured me a drink.

In essence the message to self was this:

"I prefer to expose myself as mediocre than never gift myself the experience of freely creating as I wish."

If you found yourself cringing at the word *mediocre* like many others have, we must recognize at the very least, this is how our first endeavors often start and how some of our endeavors will in fact, end. I believe this is where healthy humility comes in. This is not limiting negative self-talk. It is facing the limiting fear of actually, truthfully not being brilliant at the first go of it, after you try really hard and do your best. And knowing that it has nothing to do with your self-worth. I said to that fear, I could not care less if I find out I'm mediocre! "Well that may not be true!" People implore. You're right! And then again it may! I respond. And it's really truly okay either way. It doesn't mean I can't keep working on it, or that I won't one day be great, but we can't expect ourselves to be great coming out of the gate or great at everything we do. We just can't let that hold us back! I can't hold myself to a standard of excellence before I try. When I say that banishment of shame phrase, I'm not talking about my soul being mediocre, I was talking about trying my hand at a new skill.

Life is an experience, and that is what I want to participate in. It's about loving unabashedly, about taking risks and failing over and over again and learning each time so that you succeed in blazing a new path. Everything you will ever hear about success, whether it's spoken in the realm of career and finance or in the area of relationship and intimacy, it all has one thing in common. We must not be controlled by our fears, we must be courageous enough do work on it, no matter what comes through, over and over with the expectation to succeed. Failure is success? It is when you use it. Try, try, and try again. So, as you make choices to fill in your new life, you will need to be robust, and if you are not, life will surely supply you opportunities to become resilient. Layer by layer you will be able to shed your shame and guilt and fears, and layer by layer reach fulfillment, energy and excitement. We all know it's the journey, not the destination. I am here energetically through the pages of this book to laugh off our short-comings and help you dust your knees off when you fall. These are the joys of being human, and is actually at the very core of my unconditional love for humanity. It's in the innocent beauty of our human foibles that hook me, and our personal journeys to rise into the fullness of our power that pull on my heart strings. I empathize deeply with what it is to be human.

Communication with the Universe

We can consciously communicate with the universe to bring the person, the job, the school, the money, the house, the everything, into our lives. In this section, I have included my favorite magical, powerful, and seri-ously effective methods of visualizations, actions and invocations in a simple reference guide, mid-book to visit as needed. Speak from a pure heart and feel the presence of the universe hanging on every word. Once you have communicated your message, keep your senses open for a response. Enjoy, enjoy.

1. Yelling out loud, "I am ready!"

   You can do this to invite a significant other into your life or find a new job.

2. Radio tower and rockets of desire

   You can do this simply by visualizing erecting a radio tower that plays your message repeatedly while you go on with your life. Or shoot up a rocket of desire, a flare that catches the attention of the universe, flashing, sparkling the message of a deep desire to be manifested.

3. Visibility/ invisibility cloak

   This tool is a visualization where you place yourself in a bubble where people don't notice you. It is useful in a time of need or danger, of illegal parking, or when you would prefer not to stand out.

4. Magnetic/repellent energy

   I love this one. Imagine your energy drawing something specific in, like a sexy person or repelling something away, like mosquitos. Both are tried and tested and have amazing results.

5. Pre-sleep rituals for dream realm meetings

   Before you fall asleep you can ask to connect with and meet spiritual guiding energies for yourself. Perhaps it's a guide, angels, fairy friends, your higher self, or family and friends that have passed on to the other side. And in fact, no need to limit yourself to those that have passed on, you can just as easily connect with those who are still alive.

6. Sending thought messages to connect/disconnect

   You don't have to be sleeping to connect. Simply sending a thought to a person by thinking of them, or sending a telepathic message to them works. You can ask to cross paths with your animal spirit guides for example, or send love out to dear ones, ask babies to join the family through pregnancy or adoption. You can tell old lovers or obsessive people to let go of you. And you can send a message for a home and its current homeowners to find you.

7. Visualization of success

   Use this tool with success in sports, recitals, events, tests, just by imagining your successes, detail by detail, what it will feel like, and the sound of the swish of your three point shot.

8. Affirmations

This is a super useful tool that is broadly taught. It's worth actually learning how to do correctly, in the present tense for example in a positive statement. This practice alone is responsible for me turning around my depression as a nineteen year-old. It's powerful. What I personally learned about how it works, is that when you say a positive statement that you originally don't believe (but want to) it causes your brain to search for how SSSwhat you said *is* actually true. In doing this repeatedly over days to weeks, there comes a moment where your brain retrieves the answer, granting you an epiphany. Yes, of course this is true if I just look at it in this new way...ta da! Use this tool to become who you truly are, restore confidence and self-love.

9. Believe in being lucky in particular ways

You can decide one day that you are someone who has good weather mojo or parking fairies for example. When something comes to mind that you want to be lucky in, just say, I have good luck with such and such. I have good luck with love. I have good luck with money. It becomes your thing that just happens for you. It's pretty fun and works like a charm.

10. Relationship building with natural world

Talk with the sun, moon, stars, sky, mountains, the rivers, the trees ... You will eventually start to experience an interaction and a few magic moments of knowing that they heard you. The dimension that this creates in your life is gorgeous. I highly recommend it.

11. Healing your body with self-listening and communication

This is the work I studied only formatted as self-work. It is a simple time of tuning in and feeling sensation, the language of your body, and expressing its qualities and emotions. While tuned in, you pay attention to your mind's ear for sage messages to take forward, your mind's eye for pictures and impressions worth a thousand words that you can voice and derive great meaning, similar to dream interpretation. You can tune into the world if your body's microbiome, your body's coevolutionary co-creators, and its many populations that help us with all of our bodily tasks, that extend well past digestion. You can tune into a particular system in the body or an organ and talk to it, and voice the first thing that comes to mind as a response. It's a great form of meditation that can yield some amazing results.

12. Impulses make great leads

    What I mean by this is, you can follow flash intuitions, without really knowing the reason behind it. It can just be a compelling feeling to enter a store, or to buy something, or to pick up a phone and call a friend to see how they're doing. These are fun. You never know what you're going to get, and only half the time you find out right away, often you see the connection later on.

13. Send energy into water, plants, animals, people, and beyond.

    Send energy into water to infuse it with inspiration before serving to someone, or drinking yourself. Send energy into other beings for their health and wellness.

14. Become an empty conduit for divine energy, having no intentions what to do with the funnel of energy that comes through you, therefore making room for divine will.

These practices build your trust with the universe and make you feel undoubtedly connected to the web of life. Your experiences become fuller and deeper and decision making becomes infused with trust and knowing. As you engage more and more you can refer back to this short list to make the experiences more clear and powerful.

Preparing the mind to clearly communicate with self:

1. Recognition and or the limitation of sight-fogging fears

2. Becoming conscious of our own immediate censorship of answers to enable recognition and acknowledgement of messages you receive, especially those using words and language.

3. Discerning between your energy and that of others

Vivid visions come with practice and be prepared for immediate messages in return and responses. They often come faster than we expect, so make sure to gather all that comes with an open mind.

Communication with Self

Your emotions are the language of your spirit. An emotion, like a picture, is worth a thousand words, and should you give yourself the time to describe an emotion or a sensation in your body, you will very quickly – after about two words – run into a wall. You'll have no more words to describe and you'll stop, you know, because you're an adult and all the words that come out of your mouth are supposed to not just make sense, they're supposed to be normal. So, I want you to throw all those limiting ideas away, at the very least when you are with me and reading this book. Here, you are as yourself as you can possibly be. You say as many crazy words that come to your mind. You do wacky things, like if you are looking to unlock the meaning behind a pain in your body for example, feel free to say things like, strangling, punching, gassy, checkered or go for a fake word, like *paverment*. Hmm, sounds a lot like pavement. Just go with it. Or, if you can't get your flow on while writing chapter three because there's a little whisper over your shoulder that keeps interrupting you with critical commentary like I just experienced, you may want to stand in your kitchen and scream angrily at the top of your lungs to effing lay off and get off your own ass. The lesson to be nice as hell to yourself and stop with the critiques is a good one. If you want to move on from your situation healthy, happy and in a position to rock it, you have to be willing to do lots of things you've never done before and in ways you've never allowed. Don't worry. It will be fun … sometimes … and super interesting. And well, well worth it.

Inviting the Right Person into Your Life

There is an exercise worth doing that allows you to get very specific with what you want in a future mate. It is to simply make a list of qualities you would like them to have and keep it in a safe space or in your notebook and feel free to refine as you go. Being specific is always a must when sending desires into the cosmos.

Then I'd like you to do one more thing. Make another list that describes who you want to be to match this person. What qualities do you want to have that would complement and match your future love? Then turn your focus to becoming the kind of person that merits the things and people you want in your life. Focus on becoming your happiest and whole self, in whichever domain of your life you want most.

How I Asked for a Lover and What I Got Instead

In my own story, I had an idea I was excited about, and that was making love in such a beautiful, sexy way it would connect with divine on one end and ground me completely on the other. I had just come into this fantastic feeling of seduction and sexuality. This crazy, naughty, hot, gorgeously lingeried seductress I was, and I had wanted a partner that could hold space for it and meet me in frenzied passion. Was it even possible that someone could meet me there, willing to reach such free flying, expressive heights? I found myself from time to time asking that question. And if you do the same, do not do what I did. *Do not* spend a day looking around at people in Walmart parking lots trying to spot one. What you will see will convince you that the person you're looking for is made up and not on this planet. That was me about six months after my separation. I wanted to know lovemaking in its highest spiritual form. I had never had a sexual experience with another person other than my ex for my entire life. The last person I dated before my ex was fourteen years old! Its crazy but I think it says a lot about the position I was in, facing intimacy with another felt like filling in for Steve Carell in The Forty-Year-Old Virgin. I was excited about it in my mind, scared to death in real life.

There was a day when I was home, and I thought to myself, I am really ready to meet that person. And I decided to make it official. A note of warning: don't do what I'm about to tell you unless you really mean it. If you do, go for it. I stood at the top of my stairs in my empty house and I yelled out to the universe with all certainty, *"I'm ready!"* And, as you can imagine, the universe replied a week later, on a normal day while I was at work, seeing a client that was an acquaintance with whom I worked long ago. Never once did I think of being attracted to him, or him to me, and yet half way through the talkative session, I invited him to my friend's party to introduce him to my single-and-looking friend. Before the end of our appointment I told him that I was separated, and then for the first time ever ... I felt subtle sexual tension between us.

If I had looked at him that day while I was doing my errands around town, checking out all the unsuspecting neighbors in parking lots for their sexual prowess, I can honestly tell you, I wouldn't have recognized him as the one I was looking for.

When Juan texted me that night about some comical TV show clip unrelated to work, I knew there was a spark for him. I grinned that night over a dinner place setting for one, a playful feeling of being pleased with myself. "I got him!" I thought, and giggled. A few joke texts, followed by a few good morning messages, turning into a few all-nighters talking, making our feelings for each other palpable. The little spark became a raging fire within two weeks, and on a night I could hardly stand it anymore, he sent me a song that ignited me. At three in the morning, I jumped into my car and headed south on a long straight road to his house, all the time asking myself, "What am I doing, what am I doing, *what am I doing?!*" All I saw in front of me was a big, full, strawberry moon, saying, "Come on, come on, come on, *come on!*" Every single light on the way was green. Every door down the corridor ahead of me was open, and I followed the moon to his doorstep, on which he was sitting, waiting for me. I threw myself into his arms. We kissed. He invited me in. We kissed. We walked into the kitchen and he held me and we kissed. And we went upstairs.

I had come equipped in feeling good about my body and ready to do only what I wanted and stop if I felt like it. I had learned all these lessons and felt confident. I felt excited to express myself and always waiting for that moment that I would pull back. He was authentic, very responsive and tuned into me and I felt safe. Similar to the moon's guidance to precede, everything was just so that my body gave me the green light after green light after green light, even though I was scared out of my mind. Utterly romantic, deeply connected, and trusting was our love making. And when we found ourselves lying in one another's arms at the end, he held me and said, "You know how everyone always says that when you stop looking for someone is when you find them? I never believed them but now I know that they were right." And if making love to someone else wasn't enough to overwhelm me on ten levels, that comment right there nearly sent me into a panic. The sun had started to come up. I knew I was not going to fall asleep in his bed. I respectfully left and totally freaked out, bawling all the way home. I called my friend and cried to her.

When I stopped by my mom's house, I cried to her too. My mother held me and said, "Oh, I'm so sorry. It was that bad?" And I sobbed, "No, it was amazing, and it is definitely over!" By the way, I did break up with him immediately, only for the conversation to veer in a direction I didn't expect. He countered me, told me I had it wrong. He told me he *was* the man I was looking for. I rushed back into his arms and for another amazing night. Only to again freak out, panic, and try to end it again. It was his calm patience every time that drew me back in. What sticks, sticks. And this relationship blossomed in so many unthinkable ways. I looked for a lover and found a person prepared to move mountains, overcoming personal hurdles one after the next, and dedicated to making our relationship lasting and exquisite. Encontré mi media naranja.

I never hesitated to share my mélange of feelings with my fiancé when he dated me through my divorce. He knew what he was getting into because I told him flat out. "I'm broken," I needed a lot of space to heal and cry and grieve the loss of my marriage. It's so much to process and it takes time. It is up to us to accept this as allowable and communicate that expectation to new people in our lives. It is out of love we speak of our needs and it is love returned when others cradle these demands with gentleness and care. May you receive this generosity with gratitude and may it bring you closer.

Things can happen so quickly. When they do, it's hard to digest. You open your life to one new thing and all your fears come flying to the surface. Give yourself lots of time and patience, but allow yourself to be bold. You have good intuition. Trust your gut. It will tell you what to do, and when you feel it, follow it. If you ever feel confused, stop and ask yourself, "What does my heart say?" followed by, "What does my head say?" Do they match? Are they conflicting? I know the answer. This method is tried and true. When our minds don't see eye to eye with our inner wisdom, it all becomes a muddle. When people confuse you, did the words they told you mismatch what you felt when they said them? My loving advice, follow your heart and your gut and believe the tone, rather than the words of whatever is said. Words have a habit of holding unintentional falseness and information lacking. Feelings, rest assured, are always spot on.

Taking Action

So, what are you going to do first? What desire are you going to take seriously, make time for and invest in? Who are the people you want to invite into your life? Remember, you don't have a say when they come anyhow, so just let yourself write a list about what qualities you'd like them to have. And don't forget to create a column just next to it of the qualities you would like to exude and be appreciated for. Fold it up, put it in your jewelry box or in a book somewhere. Or just speak it out loud and run the message up an imaginary radio tower that will continue to broadcast your energy and intention into the universe.

There are so many avenues in which you can explore. The world is your oyster. Well before your separation, had you in fact set out to explore further your life's purpose, self-expression, and a sense of what you bring to the table that is unique? If so, expect to hit the ground running. As it turns out, you will be able to take all these ideas from this chapter and apply them not just for yourself, but for your children. You will see how the divorce was a necessary element required by your children in their own ways. With this insight and sensitivity to their needs, you will be able to help them benefit fully from the experience alongside yourself. You will also be able to spot a bigger trend at work, as extended family is often connected deeply in a collaborative experience of healing and evolution simultaneous to yours. We are most certainly all in this together.

CHAPTER 10

Soul Clusters

One lives inside a rather narrow viewpoint while divorcing, and everyone understands why. There's a million important details, lots of difficult conversations, lots of emotions to contend with, and your children, whom you feel responsible for dragging through this volatile time. Part of this difficulty is the sheer weight of the decision in how it affects others. So, it is very understandable why more often than not we have couples comprised of two victims, both of whom were more or less forced into the situation by the other, rather than two mutually agreeing, personally responsible individuals. In this society, the deeper understanding of why and for whom the uncoupling is happening is obscured completely, the finger is pointed by everyone, and away from oneself so not to take undeserved guilt. I will share with you the glimpses of the grand plan, that absolves all blame and that brings a sense of peace like nothing else.

There's a funny thing I've noticed time and again and it points to something quite fascinating and special. It's the idea that we move through life in little clusters of souls. Like a school of fish, we're moving in connection with one another. We enter life in a little cluster, and we often exit life alongside one another too. There's something bigger at work, encompassing circles of people and you are a part of it. This is the moment when you realize that this transformation is bigger than you. We will take our understanding a level further than most couple's conscious minds when they are moving through a major transition together, like divorce. While you and your partner are focused inward to create the changes that are required to move through this tough time, I invite you to take a quick glance at the other major shifting that is happening with the people that are connected with you, namely your children and then extend outward to your family of origin, to your extended family and your friends. I watched soul clusters at work in my own family and how it played a soulful role in my divorce.

The day this idea came full circle for me, I was at a final meeting with two teachers from my children's Waldorf school, and a team of teachers from the public school district. My son, Holden had gone through perhaps six afterschool assessments at various public schools, and with all the teammates of the local school district to gauge where he was academically, what his needs were and what kind of intervention he would qualify for. This was at the tail end of the school year before we were to head to France for the summer. I was to be in the position of choosing to either keep Holden in Waldorf where he would and receive forty-five minutes a week of free tutelage, or should I enroll him into the public school, I could receive seven hours of extra help weekly. By the end of this meeting, it was apparent that Holden could very much benefit from the extended hours of help and I was highly considering transferring him over at winter break, having already registered the children for the fall, and arriving from France weeks after public school was to start. But then, the most surprising thing happened. When the meeting ended, the school district team left, and while copies were being made for me, I sat beside the two Waldorf teachers. The tutor sitting closest turned to me, talking about the results of the assessment while winding around opinions and explanations until she abruptly ended by verbally reaching under the table to take hold of a white flag and wave it above her head. I was stunned. I looked at the peeping eyes of Holden's classroom teacher, peering just over the remedial teacher's shoulder, resembling a deer in headlights as she quickly nodded in agreement. And just like that, I had no longer a choice to continue with the school. I was uninvited to come back in the fall. My walk out of the building that day was one of crushing heart ache, which was in contrast with the sunny bright blue sky and the tall green, broad-leafed trees rustling in the breeze on either side of the subdivision streets. My heart was broken. I would miss my Waldorf School family. It had been a treasured part of our daily life. At that moment, with everything that was going on, I imagined for sanity's sake I would probably move all three children to the same public school. My time with my community of friends and my children's attendance at this anthroposophic, biodynamic school had surprisingly come to an end.

The very next day, I was called to an impromptu meeting with my youngest son, Archer's current and next year's teachers. Before I could tell them that we may not return next year, they went back on their decision to admit Archer into the first grade, after having convinced me to advance him. Sadly apologizing to me as we walked out of the room together, I was met in the hallway with a discussion of mass exodus from my daughter, Jolie's future fifth grade class, which to my astonishment had in fact just swiftly folded. I was sensitive enough to messages from the universe, which was a gift deemed totally unnecessary for this goodbye moment as the door hit my butt on the way out. Our four-year run with the dear and lovely Waldorf school had come to an end, not even as topic of discussion for Ben and me through our divorce. I knew, in an epiphany that swept through my body, that this transition was not just Ben and me making changes for the whole family. I saw my children, with their own personal paths and lives, taking hold of the next chapter alongside us. As I walked to my car, my mind flipped back to the teachings of Caroline Myss in her book *Sacred Contracts,* and I had a strong sense that on a soul level, the children, too, had signed up for this transition of divorce. I was left with a sense of comfort and awe followed by a feeling of extra responsibility to them to be sensitive to what they needed on their paths, to make all these changes meet their personal needs so they may find it positive and successful.

Have there been other huge shifts in your life and for your family?

How have your children's lives changed in unrelated ways to your divorce?

Of course, one can apply this to all of life's transitions, not exclusively with divorce. This perspective can give you a distinguishable advantage. Having this deeper sense that your children are in flow and participating with you opens your eyes to what is happening in their worlds. With this newfound awareness, you can support them in ways that truly benefit their childhoods that otherwise you may not have done. In retrospect, with regards to my own personal experience, Jolie's fifth grade year at a new school was very unique and difficult. She left with a profound level of compassion that she carried forward into middle school, where she created a world of friends and popularity boasting kindness, shaping her personality. I've never seen her so happy. For Holden, he made an unbelievable leap forward academically in his third grade class with a phenomenal team of teachers at a school that he otherwise wouldn't have attended. And for Archer, it was his relationship with his father that was paramount to his personal development. When he melted down in tantrums for no apparent reason, I was able to see into his behavior. During one of these caprices, and I asked him what was really upsetting him. He responded, I just don't know how to be a dad when I grow up. And with that, I immediately called Ben and told him he was needed, and Ben would come by and scoop him up. We made special time for the both of them to bond. Divorce often makes us better parents.

Now that we've opened up the idea that your children have their own personal soul reasons for this family transition, I want to take it one step further and suggest that this energetic weather front includes your family of origin, close friends, and extended family, clearing and evolving an entire group of people connected to the particular energy that's shifting.

If we spend a moment to think about what is happening currently with the people around us, do we see eruptions taking place? And should this have something to do with the same seismic pressures in our own lives? We may ask ourselves what is at the root of our families upheavals and does this have bearing on our situation. To clarify what I am talking about, I will share the significant moment of realization for myself and see if it resonates with you.

Years before separation, a massive karmic weather front came through my then husband's family, one that Ben had tried his very best to avoid. Eventually, after a great while of tremendous hardship, it started to surface in unfathomable ways how Ben had in fact been sewn into the tapestry of the family's secrets, prompting him to finally engage in what ultimately was the very beginning of a healing journey. I hadn't initially foreseen this soul cluster at work, or how it tied in intimately with our marital problems. This understanding came to me later on, but it provided again a deeper understanding that my divorce was bigger than me. In this case, in letting go of my marriage, I was also supporting Ben to do the personal work essential to his growth.

It's helpful to recognize and connect soul cluster work interacting in our personal lives. When we have the wisdom that widens sight to the periphery, we can see a lot more of what's going on, giving us yet another level of peace. With this, we can honor and support the process in a way that is best for everyone. As messy and destructive as the spiritual work for the soul cluster may be, this is divine clearing, opening and breaking, in order for flowers to grow in between the cracks, until beauty takes over. Tough schtuff, right? It truly is. Pain can very much be a part of growth. But can we hold all of humanity suspended in our minds for a moment and be grateful for all the chaotic, exhausting work we are doing so that we can evolve together? In this light, it is no longer possible to look down your nose and disassociate with people for the kinds of work they are doing on this planet, or down at our ourselves for that matter. It is all to be to the benefit of others, whether shared on these pages or within personal discussions or kept completely private. It is most definitely to benefit all of us, our collective consciousness, the convergent energy field in which ours extends and shares. May we often show gratitude for the person or people we know that have taken on the burden, sometimes pushing the self-destruct button to create the overdue change that their soul-pod needs, shining a light into the black ocean depths of the human spirit.

The connection we have as beings is often overlooked and not well understood in our society. This can lead to a lot of uncertainty, since in our minds without this knowledge, everyone and everything seems to hang in the balance of our decision making, taking on guilt and worry about how we are affecting others. It would feel as if the whole world is held upon our shoulders, when in fact, the world, dear ones, is suspended in space. The sheer weight of the world, which could crush you, is not for you to hold. Just try letting it go and you will see that it indeed does not fall like you would expect. Your children, to whom you likely feel most responsible through this transition, are full human beings in the beginning of their journeys, tickets paid, having entered life on their own terms. As we soften our grip on our self-oriented realities and tune into our interconnectedness, our attention turns to our children and how we may most lovingly support them in their own unique paths through childhood and beyond.

CHAPTER 11

An Environment Where Children Thrive

Your first priority is likely your children. They are the loves of your life and are central to all that you are and all that you do. How do we create an environment where they don't just survive our divorce, but they truly thrive? How do they get the most from their concurrent personal transition and strengthen their relationships with parents and siblings in the process? How do we create unshakable stability during a time of jumble and recalibration? This is the chapter that explores ideas that play into answering these questions. What do we want for our children? This is a great first question to ask ourselves and write in our journals. This will allow us to design a personalized guide for you to succeed in attaining your goals of meeting each of your children's needs, creating space for their own best personal outcomes.

There is an interesting phenomena that happens during divorce, and I don't know if you are experiencing this yet, but the sheer difficulty of the situation creates fertile ground in which your relationships become closer as you grow through it together. Of course, you have heard of horrendous custody battles and parents threatening to take full custody and sending the other parent into panic and rage. This has absolutely nothing to do with the beloved children and everything to do with vying for control and power through aggression. This will be completely avoided should we not engage in a power struggle should another initiate one. And after all that ego and threat melts down, or perhaps you've had the fortune not having to engage, or rather disengage, in futile destructive behaviors, you are left being two parents who feel the worry and sadness to lose the ability to take the time with their children for granted.

Quality Time over Quantity Time

Before now, the kids were always around ... doing something ... maybe you'd catch a glimpse of your son crossing the backyard in his snow boots, a nerf gun strapped across his back, another jammed down the front of his pants and a bike helmet on his head while you were peering through the kitchen window. Maybe they'd be tearing apart the basement toys and making lots of messes to clean up. Wherever they are, when they're not at school, they're around. This is a quite comfortable situation that falls into an everyday mode. There is less of a pressing need to deeply engage the children unless there is a problem at school or home. There is not quite the worry about bonding every day with them on a personal level like your life depends on it. They feel more like an extension of you. And so it can go, the busy day in, day out.

Then, something big happens. You move into two separate homes causing you share the time you have your chicklings in your nest. You don't get them all the time. And we get pretty upset by this.... We don't want to share. Well, a night or a weekend would be nice every so often – too bad your ex isn't a babysitter. But, no, this is they-live-with-you-some-of-the-time territory. And that's frightful. But here's the thing: You will not be able to take the time you have with your kids for granted. Little did we know this was never the truth anyways! Let's be glad to tear down that illusion. In fact, if children haven't hit middle school yet, you may not know that they wildly grow up out of nowhere much earlier than you anticipate. After separating, you and your future ex-husband realize that when they're at your house, it's special time. You enjoy. You may do more things together. You tell them you love them more, kissing them and hugging them all the time and ask all about the adventures they've had. You make it a point to make your weekend a nice one. Previously, if the other parent had been mainly focused on work and had let you do most of the caregiving for your children, that changes, slowly – it doesn't happen overnight – but in being forced to do things they've never done before, they eventually blossom. Stepping into single fatherhood can bring about many realizations, and relationships change often for the better. The trick is to be patient. There are going to be many times that you question your ex's priorities, but little by little over a few years, it's likely that you'll look back to this time and see how much they have come into their role as a dad.

Lessons From My Parents Divorce

I learned a lot in my childhood experience with my own parents' divorce when I was thirteen. People would assure me it wasn't my fault and I would say, "I know." It was assumed that the divorce itself would be traumatic for me, but I felt fine about it. In fact, I was a bit excited. I had been well aware that my mom had been unhappy, and it was my desire to see her thrive. I imagined what new step parents would be like and hoped for more brothers and sisters. I had no idea that my life would head into a time of deep sadness and pain.

My father worked and often was out on business trips. As kids, my sister and I would hide when he came home sometimes, out of nervousness I think. The memories of bonding and connection where I felt some type of affection from him I could count on one hand. The rest of the time was a sort of being-around-a-person experience. And on my other hand, I could count very sad, traumatic experiences of him harshly coming down on me for something or another. At the time my parents were divorcing, I was so close to my mother. She had promised that between she, my sister and I, we'd make a new little family – and because I felt so hurt by my father, I was ready for the next chapter spending most my time in my mother's new house, in a new town, living a new life. What I did not expect – and what ultimately became the biggest trauma coming from my parents' divorce was that my gentle mother would find (had already found) a narcissist boyfriend to take the top priority and everything else came second, destroying our closeness throughout my high school years. It wasn't until their relationship ended ten years later, as she moved into a house of her own the month before I was married, that our relationship gratefully began its return to a loving closeness.

Bizarrely enough, my father, who had never opened up to me in my life, cried as he packed a box of pictures, as he spoke to me with vulnerability trembling in his voice, about his love for my mother. For the first time I saw a beautiful a poet within him. I saw him in a new light. And he saw me in a new light too. I grew up overnight to him. And, not that we became best buddies right away, but he became my father. He saw me and I saw him. My feelings for him softened and our relationship strengthened, becoming something I cherish.

As a result of this post-divorce strain, I had a profound understanding of relationships, and the wisdom to find happiness and peace in my life, no matter the circumstances. It shaped me in ways I am forever grateful for. By age nineteen, in finding peace with my childhood, I had found realms of forgiveness and gratefulness to *all* of my teachers in *all* of their forms.

We much prefer to deliberately teach rather than bring others wisdom through trial and upset. Most of the time we do, some of the time we don't. What is important to understand is that our children will benefit from a multitude of challenges. It is physical stress that builds the density of our bones and tones our muscles after all. Feeling guilt or fear about creating unintentional hurts hinders far more than it helps. Trusting our children to find the wisdom they were intended to find and supporting them to uncover and embody strength and resilience is a much more beneficial and fine-tuned approach.

When it comes to relationships, children are quite forgiving. It is more about what is good about the relationship rather than how we fall short, and this is true for both their mother and father.

What is most important is that they feel a high quality of love. You won't be able to quantify it even if you wanted to, not with the amounts of time or money spent. It's not unlike a dear long distance soul sister friend. You may not see them so often, or even talk much, but that loving friendship is always with you. It exists in another dimension of time and space. Thinking of them makes you feel good. You feel loved. And you know, they know, you love them. So even in situations of very extreme lack, you can hold the most beautiful space between you. As hard as it is giving up time with your children, a loving mother who lavishes affection makes relationships warm and dear, and having them in your nest again makes time spent so sweet.

Motherhood has never been so precious and enjoyed.

The Desire Your Ex Change For The Better

It's a natural tendency to want our exes to be a certain way for the kids. We want them to show up for the long-distance gymnastics meets and all the teacher conferences. We want them to feed our kids healthy food. We want them to read them bedtime stories. We want them to be like us. And I will tell you with certainty that whatever you think is important for him to do, it isn't. I know, how could it not matter? If they don't eat healthy, it affects their immune systems. And you know, feeding them healthily is a way to show love. It's not responsible to feed them fast food all the time. And I say, you are right. That is a better way. And your kids will eventually thank you for not doing that. These are all fine lessons to teach. Only, that is *your* relationship. It stands on all on it's own, like a sphere of reality you help create, whole and complete.

For the first time, your ex-partner has his own sphere of shared space with the children and this takes a bit of getting used to for us. We can be too quick to point out the faults of our exes. Let me do you a favor and save you from pointless stress and potential backfire of your inadvertent reverse psychology at play. Don't point out the faults of your ex-partners parenting at all. Don't even try to influence it. Take your need for certainty and control and stick it in your pants pocket. Don't just allow, encourage the relationships between your children and your ex. Here's why: This other world of which you no longer take part in is whole, complete, personal to them and sacred, just like yours. It's has its own natural laws that govern that may be different and misunderstood by you. There will be many phases of development, shifting the landscapes of these worlds and so will change quite a bit as the natural movement of healing always comes full circle. In order to stop the focusing on what you can't control when your children aren't with you, and the stress and strain this potentially brings into all of your lives, consider the power you do have. You are fully available to support your children in handling hardships they come to you with, encouraging them to find self-supporting resolution. You are also able to discuss the needs of your children with your ex with respect in their decisions. This creates an ideal co-parenting relationship of trust, mutual respect and cooperation.

Take a moment to think about each of your children and your world between you. Feel how you come together. Sense the pull between you both. Feel the energy that unites you in this lifetime. How special and amazing is it you are the steward of this being. You have this chance to be their mother! What a most incredible, influential role. Either imagine or actually head outside to lie in the sunshine, your eyelids glowing with the warmth of the sun's rays and ponder the magnificence of this amazing opportunity you have to nurture and love on your babes.

From this place of wholeness and gratitude, you may extend this serenity by imagining the relationships between your ex and each of your children as individual crystalline spheres. Nod your head in acknowledgement of the uniqueness of them. Dig into your heart and imagine showering energy from your heart to bless the spheres you see before you. Bless them with the respect for their own paths within divinity.

Opportunities Present themselves When Children Act Out

Children thrive when their needs are met. I love Tony Robbins's practical psychology for this. And as he explains, we all have the same needs, each person's most pressing need being different and at different times in our lives. When the family is going through a huge transition like you are, their needs can slide from one to the next, as you make your way down this windy road with them. Imagine being in a car that is doing a nice sliding donut. Everything on the dash flies to the right, straighten the wheel, take a hard left, everything flies to the left. Now your kids aren't even driving the car. They don't have a way to anticipate what way the car is even going to go next, and the younger they are the less they will be able to conceptualize. You are going to have to be extra aware of their feelings and behaviors as you drive along.

If your kids are under the age of eight or nine – especially six and under – when they feel something, they *will not* be able to tell you. They don't even know what's happening yet they feel *everything*. They will act out. They'll bite someone at school. They'll get upset about putting on their seatbelt or leaving a toy at home after you back out of the driveway – the less significant the trigger is that sets them off, the louder the alarm in your head should be. Your kids are trying to let some emotion dissipate in his or her body. You see, they are not confronted with the same opportunities to let off steam. They aren't engaged in the back and forth between you and your ex, and when they feel they are, they very unlikely have any power of voice. Because their brains aren't even close to developing these communication skills, emotional eruptions occur without warning letting out all the upset, sadness, tension they energetically take on. So, things like brushing your teeth before bed or who gets to mix the pancake batter set them off. If your kids are a little older, it will sound more like: why can't I go out with friends after my band concert on a school night or, why do I have to go to school today? *Before* you address the absurdity of these questions, remind yourself of these words: this is not a real question meant to be answered. How is my child feeling at the moment? What would they get out of this if I hypothetically said yes? What is the need that underlies this distracting question? What emotions need to be released? And *this* is what you speak to and avoid the inane question all together. Get to the point. What do they feel like they need at the core and how can you work together to meet this need?

There are times when your attempts will prove futile because what's truly needed is an emotional release. Your child's nervous system might be looking to create an opportunity to melt down and get it *all* out. If this happens and you don't realize that this *is* the need being met, you will totally miss the opportunity to be supportive in their process, missing the boost in closeness. You might accidently do the exact wrong, unhelpful, isolating, hurtful thing and get frustrated and yell at them for acting super crazy.

If you've got offspring approaching or in puberty, you will likely blame it on hormones. It's so sad to do that, even though I validate the argument for it. Before you do so, ask yourself what the result will be. They will feel even more lost, misunderstood, and despairing. They'll still get out all their emotion. They were already at boiling point, sputtering out like an overfilled kettle whether you could hold space for them or not. However, if you are able to recognize it for what it is, your approach and your outcome will be so very different. For one, your understanding puts you in control. You know what's happening. They do not. You will witness and support it and feel no need to control it or make it stop. Instead you can take the surprising approach of encouraging the outflow. You will know that the emotions line up with something that has been brewing deep from within, and not engage in an argument about not getting a pizza for dinner. So instead of looking at your beautiful tortured kiddo, ready to win the holy war of logic over absurdity, you can open your heart and your arms console them of the pain of the upheaval they are experiencing at that moment. Try listening to their words as if they are speaking directly about the changes in their lives. It will give you insight into what it is that they are actually feeling and why, uncovering the mystery behind the outcry over a missing scrunchie. You could ask questions like, "What's so upsetting about not being able to find it?" And they might answer, "I just feel like I don't know where anything is anymore. I feel like my life is all over the place and I don't have a real home." *Bingo.* I can't tell you how many times I've seen parents miss these opportunities, most of the time responding to their children's wacky arguments with anger and punishments. A mid-morning text asking to be picked up early from school would likely receive an obvious, simple and unemotional, no. Fair enough, but consider that she already knew the answer and it's not what her unconscious was fishing for. She wanted to feel love and affection. I always answer those texts the same way, with a hell yeah followed by plans to head south for Mexico, beaches and backpacking adventures, and one-way tickets to Budapest. It's a no that means, I friggin' love you. I wish I could. Hang in there, cutie.

What happens when your kiddo makes a fuss, you see that there is more to it, and offer this understanding to them, placing you on their side? You come together with your young one. You have shown stability and insight at a time when everything was so uncertain for them. You have shown the ability to respond to their needs, even when you have a million things to contend with. Your child will trust they can come to you when

151

they feel a loss of control, giving you the chance to be closer with them than ever. And this simple success as a mother feels so good.

Discussing Tough Stuff That Brings Children Peace

As you move through this unraveling and reknitting process, your children will need lots of explanation. The way you explain to your children what is happening will be different based on how well they are able to understand your situation, but one thing that always is to remain the same is how honest your conversations with them are. As we mentioned earlier, when the emotion doesn't match the situation, one can assume there is more than what is being presented. This is also true in reverse, for your children when listening to you. When your words do not match the emotion or the situation, you confuse and invalidate your child's concerns instead of comforting them like you intend to. It's difficult to say the least, to explain why you're crying or why you're divorcing, or why daddy's moving out, but they can feel the energy of it regardless. What they're looking for is the puzzle piece that is missing from their logical minds. If you give them a false answer intended to comfort them but doesn't explain the emotional state you are in, they will likely take it for now, but it would create that inner confusion between mind and heart, asking them not to trust their intuition in order to believe you.

If your children are old enough or wise enough to look for the missing piece in your story, they will know you decided not to open up to them. You may think you are saving them or softening things for their own good but it's possible you're mincing words for your own comfort, when it is saving you from the difficulty of trying to explain. It is certainly uncomfortable to speak directly and openly about personal situations. In our society the common belief is to shelter children from all the emotion and all on-goings, that this somehow will benefit them. I believe children that grow up with emotionally honest and mature parents, that can cry and get upset without becoming ungrounded, help their children to become emotionally mature themselves, trusting their gut, and learn that we can get through anything that comes our way. The goal is to be as authentic as possible, to speak in their language with words that most closely translate, while *owning* your feelings. If the question is why you're crying, it's because you're really sad. If they keep asking you look to satisfy the need to know as much as possible. "I'm afraid that I'm going to not get what I want," or "I feel like I don't know what to do." I'm being general, but it won't have to include every detail, rather is it is a forthright answer true to the core of the issue. You might even notice that what you're upset about sounds a lot like what they get upset about, and you also may be able to follow it up with the solution you already know is true. It's not the situation that de-stabilizes them, it's the lack of information- the uncertainty.

Honesty is intimacy. I wouldn't ever consider getting specific about what you should and shouldn't tell your children but rather trusting your common sense and encouraging you to fill in the blank they are looking for to help them assimilate. It's all about listening to the space between your body and the one you stand in front of. Honor this space and give them the purest and truest answer. The information is handleable. Your child will start to blossom in the way of understanding relationships and psychology that will serve him or her in the future. They will grow and learn and become wise, and they may have some very wise advice for you from time to time. What is important for your child to feel is that the emotion, problem or situation present by you, belongs to you and that you are able and desiring to learn and grow from it. And for those with empathic children, I suggest that you remind them not to occupy their minds with finding a solution for you, and frame it in a way that they would be robbing you of the opportunity to solve it, which is something you want to do.

One may be equally as respectful to allowing children to champion their own problems. When they are willing or able to handle issues at hand, their confidence spikes. Listen, give advice and influence with your thoughts if you feel compelled to, but in the end make sure they leave the space feeling empowered. I often ill ask my children, would you like to handle this or would you like my help? I am happy to talk with your teacher, your father or your friend's parents. There are tremendous benefits of having beautiful boundaries in your relationships. Respecting others growth and space says, you are right where you should be in life. You are right on track. You got this. You're going to do this your own amazing way that I could never have thought of. And I'm going to be there to high five you when you see how capable you really are. This is how we raise competent, confident, self-sufficient children. This is how we raise emotionally mature human beings. And this is how we build satisfying close relationships with the people we love.

The final thing I would like to say on this matter is that, the conversation everyone is wondering how they have — the one where you tell your kids that you are in fact separating or divorcing or moving out or selling your house or all the above — by the way my kids were most upset about selling the house, surprisingly — This conversation is had the same way all of the rest of the conversations are. When we talked to our children they were the ages nine, eight, and five, my ex-husband and I were both present in the conversations with each of the three children separately. I wanted to be able to speak the right language and be attentive to their feelings and questions. We chose to do this together because it showed stability, a united front, a mutual decision, which is the truth of it in the end. It went much better than expected actually, which was weird. Our kids were concerned with how it would change their lives, but if you promise that you'll make sure things are good, they're kind of like, "Okay, well, that sounds fine enough." I think at any age when you tell your kids, their primary concern is totally personal to them: "How is it going to affect me? How does this change my life?" After all, they didn't take part in that relationship space between you and your ex. If they still get to maintain good relationships with their parents and life doesn't come crashing down, it's pretty manageable. They do, however, very much like it if you still care for each other on some level. The connection that brought you both together in the beginning, the one that sparked their existence, they want to feel that it still lives with purpose and will always have a place of honor. They have two parents. The more peacefully connected those two people are with one another the better. Nothing was a mistake, everything was sacred and full of gratitude.

It's with the respect and love of the spaces between all of us that creates the environment where we watch our children thrive. It's through intimate conversations, sharing our love and feelings in all the ways we know how and even challenging yourself to show them in new ways. The more we learn and grow through this transition the more it makes it all worthwhile for everyone. Your children set off to grow and change with you. In keeping their well-being central to our focus, they blossom- as does your relationship with

156

them. And the mothering work that is so dear to your heart expands and opens into the far corners of the universe that exists between you.

CHAPTER 12

Beating the System

There are non-standard ways of getting a divorce. This chapter is about finding your way through the legal process that gives you the best possible outcome. This guide will give you a preview of what to expect, since it's difficult to step into it blindly. I'll share with you what I would have liked to know before I filed, what I did that worked well, and what I would have done differently. At the end of this process, we want to be able to walk away unscathed, with money in our pockets, an agreement that is fair and a solid relationship moving forward with our ex-spouse.

It was after I arrived home from a summer in France that I had to get to work laying down new roots, with lots to organize, one of which was our divorce. Ben had asked me for a divorce while I was away, and my original words about it were that if he were going to ask me for a divorce that he was going to need to file and do the work for it. "I'm not going to divorce myself," I said. But in the end that's exactly what I did. It was in my best interest that we didn't stay in a stagnant place of limbo, and I seemed to be the one that had the time or ability to figure out how it was done. I started out by looking into divorcing without lawyers. I didn't feel like we needed lawyers since we were able to communicate well enough and trusted we could find an agreement between us.

There was one person in my life that really warned me not to do that. She hadn't been divorced before and tended to take extra care in protecting herself in those types of ways. To each their own. You have to do what's best for yourself and you are the best person to figure out what that is. For me, it wasn't to get a lawyer. I picked up some paperwork at the courthouse and used my friends divorce papers as a template of which I began to fill in. I would love to be able to walk you through that choice to the end, but alas, that is not how my story goes. In a conversation with Ben, I asked him his opinion about how to progress. His answer was, "Whatever is easiest and fastest." "Well," I said, "doing it myself certainly won't be either one of those things because I don't know the process." From what I saw there seemed to be a lot of ins and outs, so I opted for the next option up from there. Hire a lawyer for the both of us.

As you may well know, you can't have a lawyer represent both people. It's one or the other. Ben was okay with that. He trusted me and I honored his trust in every way I could with total transparency. I found this lawyer via my then-boyfriend, now fiancé who had been divorced ten years earlier, a former client of his ex-wife. They worked it out in a trade and it was over in a week, he recalled. However in recent years, this attorney had turned her attention to real estate, but still arranged to see me for a brief meeting and took my case. She had a retainer of a thousand five hundred dollars which I believe to be quite minimal. Ben and I split the cost at seven hundred fifty a piece. I gave her the paperwork I had started for myself, a friend's divorce agreement that I used as a template. (Doing this is a bit sad, by the way, so prepare yourself.) I assumed that the lawyer would gather information off of my template to make my agreement, but not so. She literally used the personalized template I turned in to her, proving to me that you can in fact do it yourself. I asked her for typical dollar amounts for support and rights I had. She did provide standard amounts for child support and another for maintenance. Otherwise, she gave me very minimal information, often not following up and allowing the process to stagnate. I worked with an investment advisor through the steps in transferring money over from Ben's 401k into an account for me when the time came. It was his suggestion that I ask my lawyer to get something called a QDRO, pronounced

"Quadro" where you can waive a fee to take money out of a 401k at the time of your divorce, still paying taxes mind you. She referred me to another attorney to process that, taking around two months and cost four hundred dollars. To my surprise throughout my divorce, my lawyer didn't help me negotiate anything at all or even make any outright suggestions. It was completely up to me. I submitted to her a financial agreement, as well as a custody agreement and had to complete a mandatory parenting class for the county I lived in.

Here's the hack. The more you can negotiate and agree upon on your own, the better. If your conversation is built upon a base of fairness and a desire to work together and not screw each other over, you'll come up with a better agreement, faster and much, much, *much* cheaper. There has to be that understanding between you that nurtures a feeling of teamwork and trust rather than fear that easily morphs into defensiveness, anger and bitterness. So that's what we did, negotiated on our own, mostly over the phone. We had a lot of credit card debt. I was wondering how that would be worked out through the system, and as far as I know, there's nothing that the court system does with your credit cards at all. If your debt isn't equally under your names, than you would approach that with a creative solution and that can be put into your agreement.

Ben and I set up unofficial child support starting the month after we separated. It was based on numbers I got off the internet for the state we lived in, the number of children we have, and how much it cost me not to work full time like he did. It was that arbitrary. I thought there would be hard and fast rules but I was met with total flexibility, which has pros and cons. The benefit is that you can be truly creative and work something out that is personally fair. The con is that you have to be very careful to be as giving to yourself as you are to your spouse, and that line is hard to find sometimes. It's not an emotional decision based on insecurities of either party, it's based on fairness, and sometimes you will find yourself needing to keep your boundary while maintaining compassion. Yes, easier said than done! We also separated our accounts and our bills right after separation too. This took us some time to do. When it came time to look at splitting finances, it was a tough situation without an immediate solution. He had owed me sixteen thousand dollars between half our bills I paid over the year, his portion of credit card debt under my name, a couple missing support checks and some other odds and ends. It wasn't going to be possible to pay me cash. He didn't have it. I had thought of having him pay monthly installments but this too seemed financially difficult. An important aspect to understand is that even though you are entitled to say sixteen grand as was my case, if it can't be given, you won't get anywhere simply demanding it. You have to look across the table at your friend and offer something reasonable that won't be impossible. In my case, his paying me out of pocket was not an option. You have to get really creative. I will honestly tell you the first thing I thought was, I'll just forget it. Who cares, right? It's just money. We did our best … but I am so glad that I honored myself, and the fiscally responsible and frugal decisions I had made that year. In the end, I felt so proud of the fact that I did not forgo it. I had to stand by the knowledge that my choice had absolutely nothing to do with taking from him, and everything to do with making sure I was fair with myself. And, that's when I had my idea. I gave him a call. "What if we take it out of your retirement account?" I asked. And there it was, an agreement that worked. When that money did finally come, it was a huge help in getting me off to a good start.

This brings me to a major point in discussing amicable divorce agreements. Giving everything up because you're so damn nice is *not* nice at all. There's nothing good about it. We can't pride ourselves on stealing from ourselves. What would you do if the shoe were on the other foot? That's what I asked myself. If I owed Ben money and he said to me, "You know what, never mind, money doesn't matter to me. I just don't want to put you in a tough spot," I would not accept. I would not agree to let him take the hit because I didn't hold up my end of the bargain. So, I decided to treat myself with the same respect. Why? I worked hard to make good choices that year.

I made sacrifices to get ahead. No one knew that or needed to know that but me, but how could I let myself work so hard just to tell myself I gave it away?

You *must* be fair to yourself. I know it sucks to ask for what you're owed, but it's sometimes unfair to be put in that situation as well. And if you are to work through this process with honor, you must stand just as tall for your own needs. There is no room for the martyr here. These behaviors are at their core self-serving and not a good model for your children. Not to mention that as much as I don't have a special connection with money itself, I do have responsibilities, interests and ambitions that require a healthy cash flow. Instead of giving up the money owed me, I found a solution in taking more of the 401k. And I was able to pay down the credit cards that we had managed to rack up together that were under my name. For that I gave myself a pat on the back for being fair to myself. That really helped me when I needed it.

Talk about everything, especially the hard stuff, and work it out. Think outside the box. If you are in a trusting cooperative relationship like I was, manage it outside the court system. There are quite a few ins and outs but it is definitely possible to do. We never paid more than the retainer for our divorce attorney. I did everything myself, she hardly helped and was particularly inattentive so I felt like the fee was fair, but all things considered that's exceptionally inexpensive. As far as quick, not so much. It took us thirteen months from filing to D-Day. My advice if you go with an attorney, find one that *still* specializes in divorce, and one with a good recent reference. And then I would suggest to be quite upfront with your intentions at your meeting when you hire her or him that you will be exceptionally easy as clients and that you want to make it quick and inexpensive. Ask him or her how long it will take and if you can keep it under your retainer. You will likely really have to stay on top of things. I didn't want to be annoying by being too persistent, so I was really, really nice and polite, but truthfully, I could have sat there waiting for a months before checking in, leaving a message only to receive a call a week later that they were waiting on me for something I wasn't told about. As far as I've heard, most experiences with attorneys have this disorganized feeling where they feel like their attorney wasn't on top of it and didn't do anything, only to get handed bills to the sum of five thousand dollars, and that's after they fired them to try and find someone else to get it done. I don't want to scare you, but I'd do a little homework before you hire someone.

What added some extra time to my divorce was the QDRO, and a couple extra months at the end waiting for Ben to take the parenting class that is required for my county. I'm not sure what will come up for you, just keep an open mind and know that the more you can do yourself the better. It's a little bit of a shit show.

No one really seems to know what they're doing. Also, worth mentioning is that your agreement will change in the future. With changes in employment and children's needs, schedule changes and the rest, you need a system. We have dealt with that outside the court system as well, creating a word document that we both sign and keep for our records. It's good to have things in writing. It serves both people. Memory lapse, in case you are wondering, is temporary due to stress and is likely to affect you and your ex-spouse.

And then you come to the court date, the day when legally your marriage is dissolved. I have a remarkable story of this day. I remember it quite well. I got nicely dressed. It felt strange to dress up and get yourself ready to meet your husband for your divorce. We arrived at the courthouse around the same time and we ended up walking in together. We waited for the doors to open. My attorney wasn't anywhere to be seen nor was my name on the paper by the door, so I wasn't all together sure I was in the right place. My attorney fortunately flew in just at the last minute, her wig on a little crooked, she gave me some simple instructions, and we entered. I remember the inside of the empty dark room. A judge and a court recorder, and my attorney presenting our case. The whole thing rolled out like a wedding, only the words were reversed. It brought me back to our wedding day, that happy day I married my best friend. It brought tears to my eyes. We took turns answering questions from the judge, our vows with reversed words, until the moment came where he proclaimed us not husband and wife. It was over and he released Ben and me to go take our seats once again. I turned around and tears flooded my eyes, my face tensed with sadness, and Ben sensing and sharing my tears, hugged me into him from the side and we walked back to our seats. We sniffed and caught our breath. The attorney finished with the judge and we were released. I went into a little secret side room right off the courtroom alone with the attorney to sign my name on the paperwork, one of them to take back my maiden name. She told me, in all her years of being a divorce attorney, she had never seen a divorce like mine. She was not an emotional woman, but I could sense the surprise and recognition in her voice. After some signature signing, I was done.

Perhaps it was how we allowed ourselves to stay grounded though the process that led to such a loving uncoupling. Perhaps it was how we made it a must that we don't let our insecurities and emotions drive. I believe that as unique as this story may be, I am not alone in the ability to have this experience. I believe with commitment, anyone with the desire can find beauty and meaning in the uncoupling experience. It wasn't luck. It was that I am really good at consciously setting the framework for safe space and goodwill, that allowed for both of us to show up our best selves.

Give it a go. I want to know if you managed a pleasant and meaningful uncoupling. Let me know if this book was helpful to you.

CHAPTER 13

You're Single. It's Final and Official.

This is that weird moment you step out of the court-house. It is when your life feels exactly the same as it did yesterday only you are no longer married. The emotions you have at this moment are all your own and completely valid. In my story, this is the part where we walked out together, like yep, well, I guess that's done ... we walked to our cars in the parking lot and we hugged a good long hug. He said, "I will always love you, Karinne." I told him I would always love him, too. And then he said, "So, I'll be by to pick up the kids after school today. And then it's your weekend right? And we need to get that stuff in to the school." "That's right," I said.

"Sounds good," he said. "See you later."

And there it was. Life went on. I wasn't married.

And in my sadness, I could tell my boyfriend he was no longer dating a married woman. Which, for us, was a new beginning that felt so much better and much less complicated.

This is the official moment you get to turn your attention to your new life. Everything forward from here is yours, made by you and everything you've learned up until this moment. There is a card in the tarot, the fool, that I think illustrates new beginnings quite well. It usually depicts this fool, one foot on land the other headed off the edge of a cliff. That break in the land illustrates a shift in the landscape from where you came from, to the place you're literally at this very moment crossing over into. The world you're leaving is familiar, with beliefs, rules, expectations, and a way of life that you know the ins and outs of. In the world you are leaving, you know who you are and what you do. Dropping into the next landscape puts you into a place that needs quite a bit of your attention to interpret and comprehend fully. You don't know who you are in these new circumstances and they have a way of pulling aspects forward that had been situated somewhere near the back of your personality, forward and into the light. In this new place with all this extra room for creativity, you may try your hand at something new. Super exciting! But even Mozart had to start at the beginning, which means he had to practice and learn a lot before he started to feel satisfied with what he was creating.

It's fantastic to get excited about bringing your dreams to their full potential and your skills and success to the highest mark, just know that your hard work and over-coming some bumps in the road will be well worth the effort. The new relationship that finds you, you may want to remind yourself that it takes a few years before you both really start to meld into a couple that fits, the first year or so being the hardest. But into the third year, you understand each other intuitively when you are talking. You see one another's patterns. You've resolved quite a lot of issues by then that you can have a good idea of what your relationship holds in the way of goodness. By stepping into the role of the fool one must enjoy in what there is to love about this position and also accept the disadvantages of it, if you truly enjoy this phase of your life to the fullest.

The positives about being the fool are many. It is full of excitement and growth. There is the potential for a lot of adventure, travel and going out to different events. There is a lot of room for creativity. You'll be creating a home of your own making.

The difficulties of being the fool are easy to see. It takes a while to become familiar with your new life. In the newness, there is the learning curve of it all. You have a lot of experience under your belt from which to draw, but in the situation of dating when you literally never dated before, there's sure to be some surprises! So, open mind, open heart. Hold front and center in your mind that you can't make a wrong move. Everything is an opportunity to grow and every experience you have will continue to direct you to happiness and fulfillment.

Let's make the jump together. I want you to close your eyes again and this time imagine yourself at the side of a steep cliff. Look over the edge and jump. Fall … and tell me where you land. You may while reading this instantly see the landing. What was it, on a bed of pillows or marshmallows? In a jungle clearing? A city? Even if you saw a flash of something in your mind, spend a valuable few minutes imagining your jump, your fall and your landing and your first impressions of the other side. I'll give you some advice too. This is your imagination. Do whatever you like. If you see one thing, and it seems less inventive than you like, instantly transport yourself back to the top of the cliff and make it more enjoyable to you. Once in your new world, set off to explore. What sorts of symbolism do you see? Go ahead, take a couple minutes to write them down. I'll wait!

So now that you have this impression in your mind, when the time comes where you are faced with that step out of the courthouse, or any other that feels like a, plug-your-nose-and-jump in moment, your brain can reference this joyful, carefree leap.

This phase is actually the beginning of a second phase of the divorce transition. The first part is the uncoupling, followed by the divorce and its finality. The second phase, starting the day you walk out of the courthouse, no matter how long your divorce took to become final, takes about three years. This second transition is a full physical, mental, emotional moving on from your divorce. I've seen hundreds of people over my healing career prove this general time frame to be right. This is useful to know so that you can reassure yourself that all is well. No one jumps into a new life with it all set up, ready for everything and everyone that comes your way all at once. In a culture that values productivity, time generally gives humans a lot of anxiety. As a general rule, if you are feeling anxiety and stress, check in with what time restriction you gave yourself. It could simply be unfair or unrealistic. So, by the end of this three-year timeframe, you'll feel what I'm talking about. There's going to be a feeling of resolution and peacefulness. Remember, this starts after your divorce is finalized, not after the separation. Your emotions may be a little up and down, but this is, in fact, what it feels like to be truly alive. You may measure vitality in your erratic heartbeat, that responds to every thrilling aspect, fun or challenging, that surrounds you.

The manifestation of your biggest desires and most exciting experiences will be nestled into your daily life, and it's important that you find joy in both the common and uncommon happenings. I recommend finding a daily ritual, perhaps worked into your morning routine that allows you to connect with your purpose, your goals, and most importantly what it is that you're grateful for. I like Tony Robbin's teaching about priming for the day. If your mind is a house, it's a little like tidying it up for the day so that you get the most joy from your daily life and the most progress in hitting those bigger goals that take fostering.

All the old rituals and patterns stick around for a while too. You may be driving and realize you're headed to your old house accidentally, you may call your ex in-laws mom and dad – and perhaps continue by choice, you may accidently refer to your ex as your husband. It's interesting how long it can take for these habits to disengage.

Two years after my divorce was final, I had a small insignificant phone call with my ex, and when I went to get off the phone I said quite casually out of deep seeded habit, "Love you." I totally froze on my end. Ugh. My son who was in the room looked up at me. But Ben saved the day when he laughed and said, "Well, I love you, too. Talk to you later." We all laughed and got off the phone.

Later that day, I stopped by my fiancé's work and told him and our business partner the story of what I did, ever so slightly nervous to admit I could make a mistake like that, but it didn't hold me back. I shared my awkward moment and they both laughed. It's good to knock down every barrier we can when it comes to unrealistic expectations designed to make humans behave like robots.

You create the expectations in your relationships. You lead by example of showing what is okay and what is not. We need a lot of room to grow all of us. Baby plants need big pots. Your eight-year-old needs shoes he'll fit through the summer, and you need to be able to process your feelings out in the open air, met with love. Nothing more limiting than complete freedom will do. A full healing is necessary. We are constantly recreating ourselves and thus constantly recreating our relationships. In relationship building it's important to lay out behaviors that show respect and upholding these standards is out of love. Communication is everything. And of course, it's not how much you talk, it's how well you both understand each other.

Boundaries with your ex can be difficult. They also go through this crazy metamorphosis. The moment your relationship ends, you think back, so that was the last time we made love forever ... and no, I'm not getting dressed with you in the room. It's really strange at first and there are lots of new boundaries to be put into place. As lovely as the idea may be to you to become great friends with your ex, that does not happen overnight, or even over a year. Or even over several years ... it takes as much time as it does for each of you, individually, to find wholeness and autonomy in your new life. Along the way, there will be lots of moments where you'd love it to be ready for frinedship, but your gut will tell you, it's just not time yet. Honor that. If either of you could still be wrestling with feelings, the answer to help each other out in ways you used to do, or to go out to dinner, is no, not yet. When your lives are self-sufficient, and you are both quite content, collaborate on something if you want. Meet up for lunch or extend a phone call past just kid stuff. That day will come but it isn't going to happen right out of the gate, no matter how evolved you are. This is a sacred time of separation designed to create self-sufficiency and wholeness. Take advantage of it and do things for yourself. You'll see how resourceful you are and make a lot of new friends and connections.

It's important to note that in secondary transition, your children will also be in their three year transitions personal to them. As you walk with them through this time, you can be aware of where they are in their moving on with their lives, with their interests and social lives.

Don't count down the years of co-parenting like other people do, wishing away a precious time of your children's lives. It is possible to feel good about raising children with your ex. If you can hold space for this to happen, you'll be rewarded when you work together, one day perhaps hearing some pretty great ideas come from your ex's mouth about how to handle a situation. Creating positive co-parenting space will gift you with future moments of gratitude that you had children with that person. It's worth working the soil for and planting the seed for the future.

There is room for ceremony at the end of this sacred full circle, the moment where endings kiss beginnings. You are single. Its final and official. You may have taken back your last name and you certainly feel surprisingly individual. I invite you to think about how best you can honor yourself in this open moment in your life. Your expression of the blessed fool, one leg hanging over the ledge of a world unknown as you hold a feeling gratitude for the road traveled and all it has brought to your life. May you celebrate the road ahead, certainly full of adventure and excitement of your making.

CHAPTER 14

Stepping Up Your Game

Now you can see that a cooperative and loving uncoupling is possible by holding space for both people to be their best selves. The effects of which are innumerable and far reaching, not to mention a greatly satisfying life experience for yourself. You are able to provide a nurturing space for your children to thrive, and have a sensitivity to their needs that allows you to be a truly wonderful mother. As the center point shifts in your children's young worlds, you continue a positive upbringing that you were so intent on providing for them. Conscious uncoupling allows you to not only find emotional ease during your divorce, but also saves you from the financial hemorrhage most people experience. With a clear mind-space you can focus on your new adventures, the spiritual reason you entered these crossroads. And every day now becomes a playground for you to try your best hand practicing your newfound knowledge.

This is the part where you step up your game to be your best self and honor your relationship with action that are aligned with this mission. Between your journaling and this book, we have many practices to coax you back into a optimum state of mind. You will undoubtedly get pulled out of alignment. That's the game. When you feel yourself processing your feelings and emotions and questioning your behaviors, this is the moment to fall back on what you have learned and embrace this point of power to step it up. Feeling out of flow is the opportunity to open the portal into your evolved self. Meet those moments with enthusiasm. Literally take out your hand, palm up and open your fingers, and imagine a golden invitation being placed in your possession. What does it invite you to do? Step up your game! Get into your fear and talk to it directly. What is behind it? Revisit your notes and the pertinent chapters in this book. How can you expand your perception or let go to allow yourself to move forward? In a world so full of answers for you, all it takes is asking the question. Reach out to the universe, search out some therapies or methods that get you tuned in, unblocked and get to the bottom of what is pulling you off track. The invitation was placed in your hands because you have reached the point of being able to unlock the path that takes you to a higher road of consciousness. You are armed with everything it takes to succeed in bringing you abundance in the next phase of your life.

Avoid the pitfalls that will keep you from successfully uncoupling. If you can't get over your resentment and hold onto anger or can't let go of the fact that he left you and forget the choice you made of your own, you will find a failure to progress. If you fail to recognize what part you played in your marriage that got you to the point you are now and prefer to assign blame, your children will likely suffer. Should you allow your fears to undermine your ability to take action or are self-critical, *then* it's going to be harder, longer, more expensive financially and emotionally to get divorced. Even if we saved our blame for something other than people to be nice, like bad situations, governments, societies and other outside elements, this would equally be a victim mentality and would be a way to close off creative solutions to make you feel limited and upset. And lastly, we must remind ourselves that attaching our power to our karmically connected catalyst can keep us stuck indefinitely in a difficult situation. We must get good at recognizing when we can take ownership of our emotions, including the gorgeous ones, detaching them from anything we feel could have the power to take them away.

That old seductive, comfortable place of being the victim is *really* sneaky. As seriously difficult as that may be, we don't want to assume this mentality for any reason, ever. It ultimately leads you into feeling physically painful emotions, and will unintentionally hurt the people you love most. It's imperative you take the driver seat. Assigning blame from the passenger's seat will not get anyone anywhere, though no one will blame you in doing it. There won't be anyone in the outside world that will coach you how to have a truly optimal divorce as it nearly unaccepted as a possibility. Outside this conversation there is an accepted standard, yet it slinks so far below the outcome that you want and that I want for you. It's having the courage to live with the highest standards, and connecting deeply with your motivations that will enable you to recognize the many moments it's possible to take the power back in shaping our experiences, peeling ourselves out of that victim state, thereby creating meaningful relationships and an advantageous divorce.

Remember, the tools and exercises that remediate these behaviors of self-sacrifice or self-criticism, anxiety and fear. Break the patterns that were handed down to us, that unintentionally harm us rather than serve us and that will not serve the little people we love and are responsible for. Moving into a headspace where you can be your best self opens up a reality that would otherwise simply not exist. You are your own best ally.

Why choose to do all this personal work? You will see your children learn and grow based on how you lead your life through this transition. You will see your relationships blossom. The divorce *is* the evolution of your relationship with your childhood sweetheart and will follow you into lifetimes to come, being connected through the co-parenting of your children, as well as a continued friendship in the next natural form it will take.

Even if you made choices in the past that lacked in positive communication or self advocacy, this is the time you can really step up your game! It's not an ending, it's the next chapter that is supposed to bring wealth, a deeper responsibility to your children and yourself, to make improvements you just couldn't do when you were together because you limited one another. You got this!

This is what uncoupling is all about. The rewards are immediate and awaiting you.

CHAPTER 15

Carpe Diem

The secret that you now understand is of the deeper, hidden layers of connectedness that move us in life. You see your relationships as they stretch out beyond this space and time and how we move together, clearing energies and traumas from the past. This expanding consciousness that you possess takes you beyond the standard reality and hardships that surround divorce. You shape your future through your decisions, which now come from a well of infinite imagination and possibility. And in your dance through this process, you honor and express your emotions freely all the while knowing that your choice of what to focus on and what light you cast upon your circumstances have the power to feel gratitude, security, peace and groundedness no matter what is swirling around you. In all of these domains, your personal growth, the wellbeing of your children, your marriage partnerships, and your financial health, you thrive! Of course it had never been a question of destiny. It is of your standard to strengthen your ability to show deeper love and compassion. It's your mastery of deciphering truth from fear, and your trust in knowing that where you are, right here, right now, is the fantastically exciting place to be. It is your ultimate point of power. You know that it doesn't even matter what you choose, it's why you choose it. Your decision will honor the truth in you.

As your life continues to take form with your flow, you enjoy every day for all the beauty, wisdom and nourishment it provides you, knowing that you are always moving up and onward. You meet challenges with a mindset of opportunity to test the limits of your imagination. You are finding out you are much more resourceful than you thought, as you tap into the vast collective knowing, one sphere encircling another, encircling another and one encircling that.... Always taking with you the treasures of each experience into the next phase of life. In this theatrical piece, for all the players in each of the acts with whom we interact, so much gratitude. It is the thankfulness for the people around you making this transition with you that allows you to express yourself in new satisfying ways, creating ease in your uncoupling and holds space for the shedding of your old skin and the emergence of you in your grandest style.

It is with feelings of gratitude that I have shared in this journey with you, a profound gratefulness for all the work you are doing to expand on the love this world. Yours is a life that offers example to all around of being of best service to others, shining a light that speaks of marriages being sacred even after the circle has closed and how we may always honor with whom we intensely grow.

Well done.

ACKNOWLEDGMENTS

I am in love with my team and cohort at the Author Incubator. To my friends and colleagues, blessings and gratitude. Mehrina, thank you for being there for the development of the ideas and meaning behind this first work, and your generous care and love. Moriah, thank you for supporting me when I faced my deepest fears in this endeavor and for your help to overcome them with your bright spirit guiding the way. You have been a steady stream of encouragement. To Angela, I am so grateful that you do your work on this planet and that I had the privilege in being a recipient of your channeled genius. Thank you for your benevolent spirit and killer coaching. It is because of you, this book was written.

To my spiritual support team, thank you Paula for your spunk, insight, and healing work. To Aria, thank you for your opening my eyes to the fairy dimensions and hearing the stars twinkling reply to my singing to them, so that I may live every day more deeply in appreciation. To my YouTube support team, Tony Robbins for your powerful message to live my full potential. To Steve Nobel, for illuminating my path into 5D and guiding me into the most profound meditation experiences I've ever had. To my heroes Noam Chomsky, Rupert Sheldrake, and the newest addition Theodore Zeldin for your brilliant ideas that unite people and planet. My divine encounters with the time traveler, Mike, Pete Gintz, and rose gifting John. To the generations before me whose energies were present, Marie Piat, merci et Grand-mère, que vous reposez en paix, and to the supportive spirits that surround me always, I thank you. I feel your love.

To my friends Maya and Shannon, my right-hand women that provided me everything from inspiring conversation, to cars to drive for months on end when I was out a couple, to emptying moving trucks an hour before the closing, at a moment's notice. Most the wisdom in this book came from discussions with you, taking place at any given hour of day or night. You were there for me in a way that was angelic, saving me a hundred times each. For your friendships, I am grateful to the ends of the earth.

To my family, Alissa and Mark, you help me in a way that no one else can. You are my right hand men, always there at a drop off a hat and proficient in everything. You amaze me. I can't tell you how grateful I am to you both. Socorro and Rosendo, thank you for your loving support, your care of children, puppies and home, for your endless love, and support. My children, Isabelle, Jolie, Christian, Holden, and Archer Finn. I love you more than life itself. You are my treasures. What a pleasure it is to see you all come into all your talent and beauty every day I have the pleasure to spend with you. You are the inspiration for reaching higher and further than ever before dared.

And finally, an extra special thank you to Juan, for such loving and attentive support, for bringing me copious amounts of "pan," your patience and gentleness. May I be so blessed to wake up to your beautiful sappy face all the mornings the future gifts me. Thank you for rearranging your life to take care of everything, so that I could dedicate time to my best effort in being of service to my dear readers. *Te amo tanto.*

ABOUT THE AUTHOR

Karinne Piat is an intuitive healer, uncoupling coach, and author of *The High School Sweetheart's Survival Guide to Uncoupling*. She lives in the suburbs of Chicago, having spent nearly two decades facilitating health and wellness of physical, mental, and emotional trauma with a practice of CranioSacral, SomatoEmotional Release, and massage therapies, refining her skills in clairsentience, clairvoyance and inter-dimensional adeptness. She knows intimately the human body and speaks its language of sensation, emotion and imagery. She enjoys teaching her clients proficiency in the language of their own bodies, to reach one's full potential of health, happiness and wellbeing.

After Karinne's marriage to her high school sweetheart surprisingly ended and home life with their three children drastically changed, she sought to share the insights and epiphanies of her conscious uncoupling experience with those suffering such a loss. She believes that marriage has changed considerably in this new era, bringing a shift in what is possible for couples facing divorce. It is with understanding the profound nature of childhood sweethearts and the unique challenges they face that she wrote **The High School Sweetheart's Survival Guide to Uncoupling**. Through personal coaching, healing, and self-discovery retreats, she works to be of best service to others that find themselves in the same unique position, creating space for simplicity and peace within in the context of their divorce.

ABOUT DIFFERENCE PRESS

Difference Press is the exclusive publishing arm of The Author Incubator, an educational company for entrepreneurs — including life coaches, healers, consultants, and community leaders — looking for a comprehensive solution to get their books written, published, and promoted. Its founder, Dr. Angela Lauria, has been bringing to life the literary ventures of hundreds of authorsin-transformation since 1994.

A boutique-style self-publishing service for clients of The Author Incubator, Difference Press boasts a fair and easy-to-understand profit structure, low-priced author copies, and author friendly contract terms. Most importantly, all of our #incubatedauthors maintain ownership of their copyright at all times.

Let's Start a Movement with Your Message

In a market where hundreds of thousands of books are published every year and are never heard from again, The Author Incubator is different. Not only do all Difference Press books reach Amazon bestseller status, but all of our authors are actively changing lives and making a difference.

Since launching in 2013, we've served over 500 authors who came to us with an idea for a book and were able to write it and get it self-published in less than 6 months. In addition, more than 100 of those books were picked up by traditional publishers and are now available in bookstores. We do this by selecting the highest quality and highest potential applicants for our future programs.

Our program doesn't only teach you how to write a book – our team of coaches, developmental editors, copy editors, art directors, and marketing experts incubate you from having a book idea to being a published, bestselling author, ensuring that the book you create can actually make a difference in the world. Then we give you the training you need to use your book to make the difference in the world, or to create a business out of serving your readers.

Are You Ready to Make a Difference?

You've seen other people make a difference with a book. Now it's your turn. If you are ready to stop watching and start taking massive action, go to http://theauthorincubator.com/apply/.

"Yes, I'm ready!"

OTHER BOOKS BY DIFFERENCE PRESS

Reverse Button™: Learn What the Doctors Aren't Telling You, Avoid Back Surgery, and Get Your Full Life Back by Abby Beauchamp

Never Too Late for Love: The Successful Woman's Guide to Online Dating in the Second Half of Life by Joan Bragar, EdD

Stronger Together: My MS Story by Chloe Cohen

Yogini's Dilemma: To Be, or Not to Be, a Yoga Teacher? by Nicole A. Grant

Come Alive: Find Your Passion, Change Your Life, Change the World! by Jodi Hadsell

Meant For More: Stop Secretly Struggling and Become a Force to Be Reckoned With by Mia Hewett

Lord, Please Save My Marriage: A Christian Woman's Guide to Thrive, Despite Her Husband's Drunken Rants by Christine Lennard

If I'm so Zen, Why Is My Hair Falling Out?: How Past Trauma and Anxiety Manifest in the Physical Body by Amanda Lera

Heal Your Trauma, Heal Your Marriage: 7 Steps to Root, Rebound, and Rise by Dr. Cheri L. McDonald

WELCOME to the Next Level: 3 Secrets to Become Unstuck, Take Action, and Rise Higher in Your Career by Sonya L. Sigler

Embrace Your Psychic Gifts: The Guide to Spiritual Awakening by Deborah Sudarsky

Leverage: The Guide to End Your Binge Eating by Linda Vang

Under the Sleeve: Find Help for Your Child Who Is Cutting by Dr. Stacey Winters

THANK YOU!

I am so grateful to connect with you through this book! I hope that I was able to help in some special way as you navigate this difficult but sacred time of uncoupling. Should you desire further personalized guidance through programs, workshops, or upcoming events, feel free to email **karinnepiat@gmail.com** for more information, and feel include any comments, questions, and thoughts.

Love and Blessings to you and your family!